The Rookies Guide to Block Wars

Matthew Sprange

Contents

Credits

Editor
Alexander Fennell

Cover Art
Greg Staples

Interior Illustrations
Nathan Webb (49, 53), John Caliber (41-42, 44, 52, 54, 56-57, 59-61) Emberton (3, 4), Mike McMahon (6-20, 22, 24, 27-28, 31, 37, 45, 47, Ron Smith (5, 32, 36)

Graphic Design
Anne Stokes

Proof Reading
Ian Barstow

Judge Dredd created by John Wagner and
Carlos Ezquerra

Introduction

Over 400 million citizens are housed within Mega-City One, with every need met by the hard toil of a billion robots and the ever watchful Justice Department. The vast majority enjoy a life of pure leisure, pursuing any number of hobbies, interests, sports or crazes in an effort to keep their minds occupied and just have something to *do* from day to day. The Tri-D stations cater for every conceivable taste and the great corporations endlessly churn out millions of new and exciting products knowing all too well that, for some citizens, shopping is as much a legitimate pastime as anything else.

Life is far from perfect, however. Sheer boredom of an existence filled with nothing but leisure time is the single greatest contributing factor to crime. Combined with intense overcrowding in mile-high cityblocks, few citizens remain completely sane throughout their lives and there seems to be no limit to the violence and terror that they can inflict upon the rest of the population of the city. Civil unrest is a regular feature of Mega-City One and even the most mild-mannered citizen harbours a deep-rooted loyalty to the cityblock in which he has lived his entire life. Every other block is, in some way, inferior, being either too run-down, too snobby, too aggressive, too impolite or too tall.

Block fighting is a common feature of life in Mega-City One and most citizens can expect to be caught up within one at some point during their lives. Boredom, overcrowding and mass unemployment all combine to set tensions on a razor's edge and the slightest incident can spark off a block war within minutes. Once two blocks begin waging war upon one another, the judges must act quickly to contain the violence before it spreads. Battles involving several blocks can quickly spiral out of control as the Citi-Def in neighbouring cityblocks watch the escalating combat and argue which side they should join. Left unchecked, a single minor incident can spark off a war that envelopes a dozen blocks and claims the lives of hundreds of thousands of citizens in less than an hour. Whenever such incidents occur, it is the sworn duty of every judge to put down the unrest as quickly, efficiently and brutally as possible. Any reluctance can only cause the deaths of more citizens.

The criminal elements of Mega-City One, however, greatly enjoy the prospect of a mass block war. With the judges' attention diverted elsewhere, incidents of opportunistic looting, robbery and related crimes increase tenfold for miles in every direction around the warring blocks. The greatest perps may actually instigate a block war intentionally, as a key part of a crime that will perhaps net them millions of credits. With a hundred thousand citizens rampaging through the streets, crime bosses have in the past utilised the mob as a hapless army to be thrown against the defences of a Justice Department armoury in prelude of a raid to steal high-powered weaponry, or alternatively as a simple distraction to keep the judges away from other planned crimes. The possibilities for perps using block wars to their advantage are endless – it just takes a skilled criminal mind to plan for them.

The Rookie's Guide to Block Wars

This rules supplement is a comprehensive guide to block wars, rumbles and riots in Mega-City One. It presents players of citizen characters in perp-based campaigns with a whole new dimension with which to wage war against rival street gangs or the Justice Department itself. Players with judge characters can now take part in the infamous block wars of the city, specialising in the riot squad or taking advantage of new and greater ordnance with which to combat vast numbers of rampaging citizens. Games Masters will find they have a wide variety of new tools to use when presenting one of the most dynamic scenario ideas to have appeared in the 2000AD comic strip – your players may be fairly relaxed when their judges arrive at a bank to halt a heist in progress, but when faced with a mob one hundred thousand strong, they might find their tactics have to change radically.

The mass combat system presented within *The Rookie's Guide to Block Wars* has many uses, some of which are covered in Chapter 7. As well as giving a fast and comprehensive system for conducting block wars, riots and rumbles between rival street gangs, Games Masters can now also fight entire battles or even wars amongst the different mega-cities or alien races.

The streets have just become a lot more dangerous. . .

Riots and Block Wars

Mass civil disturbance occurs everyday in Mega-City One, driven by the vast overcrowding of the population and high unemployment rates. Citizens may rally against the lack of jobs, the authority of the judges or the death of a well-known Tri-D soap character – it does not take a lot to trigger a mob instinct that can result in thousands of deaths and millions of credits-worth of damage. Every sector suffers, though some have a disturbing reputation for both the regularity and intensity of riots and block wars that rampage through the streets. It is the nightmare of every judge on the force to be confronted with one hundred thousand rioting citizens without available back up and many study hard in preparation for the day on which they may find themselves in exactly this position. Judge Dredd has the power, reputation and authority to arrest an entire block but this is an option few judges are able to successfully exercise and most die trying. Only a combination of teamwork, back up and sheer courage may see a judge through what is probably the very worst Mega-City One can throw at him.

This chapter takes an in-depth look at the different types of mass disturbance faced by the Justice Department and the methods by which they are commonly dealt with.

gangs are forged and broken, and increasingly heavier weaponry and ordnance is brought into play as the stakes rise.

Many judges may be tempted to simply leave street gangs and juves to tear themselves apart, though any experienced judicial personnel will advise that this is an extremely hazardous course of action. Things may seem safe enough as perps hammer each other into unconsciousness in some deserted part of the sector but all too quickly firearms and heavy weaponry may be brought into action and the rumble can spread unbelievably quickly into crowded population centres. A rumble can cause a significant amount of collateral damage as both property and innocent citizens get caught up in a lethal crossfire.

What may start as a simple knife fight between two gang leaders to determine who has right of access to a munce burger bar, hideout or pedway can quickly devolve into a mass brawl. As firearms are brought out, the death toll rapidly increases. Other juves and street gangs may join in, carefully picking their allies and unleashing everything they have at their enemies. If judges are not called to the scene in very short order, vehicles, bombs

Rumbles

Typically the preserve of juves and young punks, a rumble is the description commonly given to any running street fight involving one or more sides targeting each other. It is also the term applied to the regular small-scale battles that take place between rival street gangs seeking to force one another from an area. Rumbles are relatively small affairs usually involving less than one hundred citizens on each side, though the sheer amount of damage that can be caused far outweighs the number of combatants. The gangs taking part are often deadly rivals looking for the slightest excuse to go to war and destroy their long-term enemies. Because of this, rumbles take on an incredibly personal edge and can escalate rapidly as temporary alliances with other

MANTAS HERD OTHER SCATTERED BANDS OF JUVES INTO THE GROWING STAMPEDE –

Department is that such complaints tend to become self-perpetuating and what might start as a tirade from one citizen against all the unfairness in his life can soon develop into an illegal parade of thousands of citizens. Once this many are on the move, all simultaneously demonstrating against the same perceived injustice, trouble is inevitable. This is the reason the Justice Department grants very few permits for parades and ruthlessly quashes those that spring up without their authority – it has little to do with a distrust of any democratic system (though that is very much another story) but simply indicates that citizens cannot be trusted to take to the streets in any great numbers.

A riot can develop for reasons that, in the aftermath, may seem incomprehensible, even for the citizens involved – though this is no excuse for their lawless behaviour. A desire for democracy and the end of the judge system, housing rights and anti-alien protests have all been the cause of massive riots throughout Mega-City One in the past. However, so has the withdrawal of a certain brand of synthi-bar, the change of broadcast times for a Tri-D game show and the repainting of a cityblock. Mega-City One is a tinderbox of differing interests, prejudices and dissatisfied citizens, all looking for an outlet for their frustrations. Many may not even agree with the protest in which they are marching but they are all too willing to go along with the masses simply as a release. It has even been known for riots to change the target of their protest several times during a march, as several particularly charismatic citizens alternately take the lead for short periods of time. This can leave judges preparing a response a little bewildered as the riot literally takes a turn for the worst. The citizens engaged in the riot, however, may not even notice they are now fighting for a completely different cause.

Riots pose particular problems for the judges as they tend to be mobile affairs and can cover several miles before being properly contained. As the riot travels, more and more citizens are drawn into the violence as it takes a life of its own. The citizens within riots rarely target one another, unless a dispute in views of doctrine becomes evident, but they can cause an incredible amount of damage as vehicles are over-turned and burnt out, blocks

and missile launchers may be unleashed into the carnage, threatening everyone nearby. However, judges should be warned that the participants of rumbles are notoriously fickle, especially if they are comprised in the main of juves. As soon as the judges arrive in force, the combatants of the rumble may well unite almost instantaneously against the judicial response, forming temporary alliances in order to battle against the force they all truly hate – the Justice Department.

So long as experienced judges arrive on the scene of a rumble quickly, they can usually be contained within minutes, and for those who lack Judge Dredd's impressive authority, a single Manta Prowl Tank can instantly quell any such disturbance. All that will remain is to identify the gang leaders, sentence all lawbreakers and detail clean-up squads to deal with the mess that remains.

Riots

Citizens enjoy complaining for it is one of the few legal pastimes that costs no credits. The danger for the Justice

are attacked and shopping malls looted. The more serious riots actively target a perceived enemy or threat, such as a particular race of aliens, gang of juves or chain of kneepad stalls. When this happens, an ugly witch hunt can develop, with mob justice being executed against possibly innocent targets in a hideous fashion only witnessed in the Mega-City.

For these reasons, riots are given the highest priority for response by judges. In theory, a riot left unchecked could travel through an entire sector, raising every citizen up in arms and leaving utter carnage in its wake. Unless the entire city is in the grip of a new, revolutionary and potentially dangerous idea (such as the democracy riots of 2113), riots tend to be limited to a few thousand angry citizens, though it is only the presence of the judges that stops them spiralling further out of control.

Block Wars

By far the most well-known of all civil disturbances is the block war, though rumbles and riots tend to be more common. The cityblocks of Mega-City One are monuments to human ingenuity – rising over a mile into the cloudless sky, each housing tens of thousands of citizens, jam-packed together as part of the space saving measures necessary in the overcrowded city. Every possible convenience a citizen could dream of can be found within his own block, including shopping malls, bars, leisure centres, hover car showrooms, med-centres, arcades, and much more. It is possible for a citizen to live his entire life without ever needing to leave his cityblock – and many do just that. An unfortunate side effect, however, is that it is all too easy for a citizen to start imagining a loyalty to his block, the idea that, in some way, his block is a far better place to live than any other. This breeds a natural rivalry between the citizens of neighbouring blocks and while the outward signs of this are usually little more than juve gangs preying upon one another, it can ignite into full scale warfare.

The incidents that have precipitated block wars in the past could be laughable, if their consequences were not so tragic. It is generally believed that the greatest block war in the history of Mega-City One was caused by a four-credit Freezy-Whip being dropped on to the head of a citizen of a

rival block. A far more common cause is to be found within the Citi-Def units present in every block. Bored with countless training exercises and mock combats, the part-time soldiers of the Citi-Def units yearn for real battle or 'trigger time', as they call it. The most obvious target is, of course, the Citi-Def soldiers of a neighbouring block. It does not take long for ordinary citizens to join their Citi-Def in attacking a rival block and, with the incredible weapons to be found in their armoury, an immense amount of damage can be caused before the enemy has time to react. Missile launchers, lazookas and missile defence lasers can all be turned upon fellow citizens as the battle intensifies.

Block wars can involve hundreds of thousands of citizens and judges must move quickly to segregate warring blocks before their neighbours also become involved. The death toll of even a short-lived war can be catastrophic as high explosive shells and piercing high-intensity lasers pound each block to rubble. In rare events, Citi-Def units have infiltrated the foundations of

THE SMALLEST OF THINGS CAN SPARK A BLOCK WAR — EVEN SOMETHING AS INNOCENT AS THE DROPPING OF A 4-CRED **FREEZY-WHIP** —

SPLOT!

YOU DIRTY FILTHY BLYTON BLOCKERS! YOU DID THAT ON PURPOSE!

MELDA DREEPE HAD BEEN FEELING AGGRESSIVE ALL DAY. SHE WAS NOT THE ONLY ONE. WHEN SHE ENTERED HER BLOCK, **DAN TANNA**, A CHILL OF BARELY-RESTRAINED VIOLENCE RIPPLED THROUGH THE AIR —

the iso-cubes as the judges haul thousands of perps off to complete their sentences.

Sector Wars

Incredibly rare in the history of Mega-City One, full-blown sector wars can make even a multiple block war seem insignificant. As a rule, citizens are far less devoted to their sector than they are their own cityblock though, once again, it takes little to trigger the mob instinct present in all of them. Sector wars involve millions of citizens, all mobilised under a common banner against their enemies in an adjacent sector. Battle lines can stretch dozens of kilometres, with each army led by the combined Citi-Def units of all the blocks in the sector. The potential for destruction and carnage is incalculable and the Justice Department will move swiftly to defuse the crisis.

One of the most famous examples of a neatly averted sector war was started by the civil councillors of Sector 1. The power supplies for their entire sector were being constantly disrupted by peak-time overloads from the neighbouring Sector 3. Unable to resolve the dispute to their satisfaction, the councillors illegally mobilised every Citi-Def unit in the sector. In less than an hour, Sector 3 had responded and two immense armies faced one another across a fifteen kilometre front. Judge Dredd was dispatched to avert the brewing sector war, a task he accomplished by cutting off the power to both sectors until every Citi-Def unit had dispersed back to their own blocks. The councillors of both sectors were subsequently arrested by Dredd.

Causes

It is a common joke among judges that citizens need no reason to go to war with one another and, indeed, the surface reasons for block wars and riots can seem incredibly trivial when exposed to detailed examination. The fundamental causes, however, are always the same. Mega-City One is a population centre in a permanent state of crisis. The succession of disasters to plague the city have left many completely homeless and those lucky enough to be catered for by the Housing Department are

their rivals, planting mega-explosives designed to bring the block crashing to the ground, prompting the Justice Department to mobilise every emergency squad in the sector.

The judges of any given sector may expect to face a block war perhaps once each month on average, though some sectors are notorious black spots of disillusioned citizens just itching to take their frustrations out on their neighbours. Few cityblocks are actually destroyed by these block wars but deaths will always run into the thousands and the cost in criminal damage can rise to millions of credits, to say nothing of the burden placed on crammed into tiny apartments among tens of thousands of other citizens. The proliferation of computers and robots in industry, while making for an extremely efficient economy, has driven unemployment to stratospheric levels and literally given citizens far too much time on their hands. As Mega-City One spirals downwards under increasingly severe crime waves and social disorder, the judges alone stand between relative peace and total anarchy.

A more disturbing trend in recent years, however, is that of the intentional block war and riot. Due to the massive numbers of citizens involved in these disturbances, the response of the Justice Department will always be of a similar magnitude. In a time where the resources of the judges are severely limited and a massive shortfall in manpower exists, this means that one block war can all but drain an entire sector's ability to respond to other crimes. This filters down to all levels. While it is standard practice to increase judge visibility within a one mile radius of a block war or riot to discourage opportunistic looting and other crimes, this can seriously impact a patrol of street judges on the other side of the sector who may well find absolutely no back up units are available to them when confronting even major criminal activity.

Perps have begun to learn this flaw in the Justice Department's policing methods and the best of them use it to their advantage. When planning raids on high-value facilities such as banks and Justice Department armouries, some criminal organisations will seek to intentionally start a riot or block war a few miles away in order to both draw judges away from the intended target and cripple their ability to respond while the crime is in progress. Unfortunately for the perps, while riots and block wars can start with the most minor provocation, months of planning can go wasted as they slowly begin to realise that citizens are a fickle race. One badly chosen phrase from an eldster to the wrong juve can spark a whole block war but things can quickly become more problematic when perps try to intentionally start a disturbance. It can be irritatingly difficult to tap into the group consciousness of tens of thousands of citizens simultaneously and just as the Justice Department can find it nigh on impossible to predict where the next block war will take place, so can perps find it amazingly difficult to start one deliberately.

THE SEETHING MASS OF BLOCKERS **PARTED** BEFORE THE JUDGES' AWESOME FIREPOWER –

AIEEE!

Block wars and riots are spontaneous events that have so far defied rational and scientific analysis. Many perps and criminal organisations are far more content to simply bide their time and launch their operations when a block war develops by chance. They are unlikely to have a long wait.

Judicial Response

By necessity, the response of the judges to riots and block wars must be swift and total. The citizens they are sworn to protect can easily escalate a minor situation into a major tragedy and so a certain ruthlessness is required by judges arriving on the scene as a block war begins to flare up. The use of Stumm Gas is automatically sanctioned for it is far better to face a tiny proportion of deaths from allergic reactions to the toxin than thousands of casualties later on. Riot foam may be used to flood entire plazas in an effort to keep the mob from fighting and, in extreme cases, sonic cannons can be turned upon the blocks themselves to immobilise their citizens. Major ordnance is also likely to be deployed, for the longer a block war rages, the more damage will be sustained in the surrounding area and the more judges will be tied up dealing with just this one incident. Pat-Wagons, H-Wagons and Manta Prowl Tanks are therefore all made readily available, where possible, once a street judge calls for back up.

Specially trained and equipped riot squad judges will also be deployed in sectors that keep them on permanent alert. Often disregarded by street judges who view riot squad duty as somehow second-line when compared to fighting crime directly, these judges are actually superbly disciplined and well versed in handling numerically superior opposition in a manner designed to pacify rampaging mobs, rather than incite them to further violence.

Given enough warning from narks, the Wally Squad and other informants, judges are also empowered to put entire blocks under solitary confinement where it is believed a block war is imminent. This is a method by which the blocks are quite simply shut down from the rest of the city, with no citizen being permitted to enter or leave until the Justice Department raises the blockade. This has little impact on the majority of citizens in such blocks, for everything they need in day-to-day life can be found within but, by separating them from their neighbours, extreme violence may be averted.

All too often, however, no such alert is available to the judges and those on the street may literally find themselves walking into a war zone with little or no warning. In such circumstances, judges are advised to keep their distance until back-up arrives for even their superior training and equipment will avail them little against a mob one thousand strong.

The Aftermath

Once the perpetrators of a block war or riot are arrested and sentenced, and the clean up squads have been and gone, it is the lone citizen who has to cope with the aftermath of destruction. It is likely he will have lost friends and family in the fighting and will probably hold a deep-rooted grudge against the rival block, one that the judge's solitary confinement of his own block cannot shake. He may not have released all his pent-up frustration before the judges arrived and will have to face yet another day of boredom and unemployment – it is a well known fact among med-judges that incidents of Future Shock Syndrome can double among the survivors of block wars.

The Justice Department keeps an extremely close eye on blocks that have warred in the past and rivalries can be maintained for many years. In general, this friction is restricted to juve gangs from the two blocks engaging in isolated rumbles but there is always the fear that a full-scale block war may erupt once more as citizens on either side start gearing themselves up for a re-match – usually led by their own Citi-Def unit. Regardless of its past history, each block within Mega-City One must be regarded as a potential trouble spot for riots, block wars and worse.

ELECTRO-CORDONS WERE HASTILY THROWN UP TO CONTAIN THE AREAS WORST HIT –

CRACKLE ON!

Block Mania

Even by the year 2103, block wars were nothing new to the citizens of Mega-City One. The judges knew that inter-block violence could erupt at any time and were well-trained in handling block wars. However, nothing could have prepared either the judges or citizens of Mega-City One for Block Mania, the day when the whole city went wild and almost the entire population succumbed to a madness created by East-Meg One that was to result in the destruction of nearly half the city.

It is generally agreed among the judge-tutors of the Academy of Law that Block Mania began with a small enough incident – the dropping of a 4-cred Freezy-Whip

on to the head of Melda Dreepe, a resident of Dan Tanna, as she walked past the Enid Blyton cityblock. During any other day, this may have caused Melda some consternation but would otherwise have had no lasting effects. Unknown to the judges, however, Block Mania had already seized the citizens of Mega-City One and they were just looking for an outlet that would allow them to unleash their collective and barely-restrained aggression. Melda returned to Dan Tanna to attend an overcrowded block committee meeting where the decision was made to start a full-scale block war. Melda Dreepe's lightning-fast proposal of Enid Blyton for the target was greeted with unanimous approval – within an hour, the Dan Tanna Citi-Def unit had planned a frontal assault and was leading almost every citizen of their block across the plaza to Enid Blyton.

It was perhaps unfortunate for the residents of Dan Tanna that their counterparts in Enid Blyton were ready and willing to make war – the first deaths as a result of Block Mania came as the Blyton blockers unleashed their full Citi-Def arsenal into the charging Dan Tanna mob. Judges, led by Dredd himself, soon arrived on the scene and halted the battle by flooding the corpse-strewn plaza with two entire Pat-Wagons' load of riot foam. It was unfortunately too late and Block Mania had already spread beyond Blyton and Tanna.

Neighbouring blocks, their citizens all charged with the same naked aggression that had swept through Blyton and Tanna, had been watching the developing block war with interest. Rikki Fulton and Henry Kissinger blocks sided with Enid Blyton. Betty Crocker had chosen to ally with Dan Tanna while the citizens of Pancho Villa were fighting everybody. Judge Dredd and his colleagues soon found themselves caught in the middle of a six-block war. The standard procedure for dealing with any mob was to target the leaders but this time such tactics were to prove fruitless –

AT 02.30 THE ASSAULT WAS LAUNCHED –
DAN TANNA! DAN TANNA!

THE ENID BLYTON BLOCKERS WERE WAITING. THEY TOO HAD FELT THE TENSION OF THE DAY. SOON IT WOULD FIND RELEASE –

THOSE DUMB TANNAS! WALKIN' RIGHT INTO OUR EVER-LOVIN' ARMS –

LET 'EM HAVE IT!

fallen agitators and Citi-Def officers were simply trampled underfoot as one of Dredd's Pat-Wagons was overrun and wrecked by the combined strength of the charging citizens. Surrounded on all sides, the judges had no choice but to turn their bike cannon on the mob and literally blast their way to freedom.

Behind them, the block mobs met like human battering rams, smashing one another apart. The remnants of Dan Tanna fought close beside the Betty Crocker blockers. Arrayed against them was the concerted might of Henry Kissinger, Rikki Fulton and Enid Blyton, with Pancho Villa taking on all comers. By this time, well over three hundred thousand citizens were involved and fighting had spread far beyond the central plaza. Judge Dredd ordered the immediate deployment of Stumm shells from his remaining Pat-Wagon, being only too willing to accept deaths from the allergic reactions of the gas rather than let the mobs murder one another. Pancho Villa responded by destroying the Pat-Wagon from the top of their own block with a recently acquired missile defence laser, which was quickly silenced by Dredd himself.

By this time, many separate block wars were beginning to spread throughout the northern sectors at an alarming rate. Chief Judge Griffin placed Dredd in charge of the operation to crush the block wars before they spread throughout the entire city. It was to be a hopeless task.

Block wars continued to erupt through the northern sectors and many smaller engagements began to flare up.

An army of mo-pads laid siege to Garner Ted Armstrong block while ten thousand warring blockers perished when the overzoom they were fighting across was destroyed by mega-explosives. Now on board an H-Wagon observation craft, Judge Dredd had recognised a far more worrying development – many judges in the northern sectors were also beginning to succumb to the same madness overtaking the citizens. The judicial system began to break down as station judges tried to decide which blocks they would fight for! Beginning to suspect an outside agency was responsible for Block Mania, Dredd ordered forensics squads to start performing complete rundowns on arrested citizens.

Under Dredd's command, the judges on the street fought hard to quell the Block Mania. By now, every canister of riot foam in the entire city was in use in the northern sectors. However, even with this added support, both riot foam and Stumm gas stocks were dwindling to dangerously low levels and still the judges faced overwhelming numbers. Electro-cordons were hastily erected to contain areas of the heaviest fighting but while they managed to throw back citizens charging their containment field, all too often another block war would erupt outside of the new perimeter, forcing the judges to pull back even further.

More trouble seemed inevitable when Judge Dredd was approached by his top informer, Max Normal. Max reported that the citizens of his block, Ricardo

Montalban, had discovered the toxic properties of a combined cyclic acid and raw plasteen compound, and were planning to create enough poison gas to wipe out a thousand cityblocks. It was also apparent that Max Normal was not affected by Block Mania and while Dredd led a squad to deal with the threat of mass murder, he was taken away by forensic squads for a whole battery of tests to determine just why Max Normal was so normal.

By this time, inter-block war was now total throughout the northern sectors – every block had succumbed to the madness and Block Mania reigned. In the devastated Dan Tanna block, where the fighting had begun earlier during the day, a few surviving residents were still fighting. They had been Stumm-gassed, riot-foamed, bombed, blasted and arrested. Out of an original population of over 70,000, only 277 remained alive and at liberty. Melda Dreepe was still fighting and she had become the nominal leader of Dan Tanna. Looking around the battlefield, she made the decision to lead her dwindling forces in an assault to capture Rikki Fulton block.

Further east across the city, Ricardo Montalban blockers had secured an alliance with luxy-block Charlton Heston. The Heston blockers were detailed to capture several acid tankers and deliver them to the Dixy Plasteen Complex, where the Montalban Citi-Def were already launching a full scale raid to obtain tonnes of raw plasteen for their diabolical plan to wipe out their fellow citizens.

Judge Dredd and his squad arrived in time to halt the last of the acid tankers entering the plasteen complex but it was too late for the manufacture of the toxic gas had already started and the chimneys of the complex began to churn out roiling clouds of the death gas. Weather control was called in to deal with the gas cloud by creating an artificial cyclone to suck it skywards, while Judge Dredd brought in sonic cannon to raze the complex to the ground. Weather control finally managed to avert catastrophe but it was far too late for the closest blocks. Among the dead from the toxic gas were Melda

Dreepe and the remaining Dan Tanna blocks, caught in the open when the lethal cloud swept over them as they charged towards Rikki Fulton.

By now, it was clear that Block Mania had a firm grip on over 150 million citizens. Having no other choice, Judge Dredd ordered the pacification of every northern sector of Mega-City One. Sonic cannon moved in and began targeting mobs with low frequency wide beams. Each blast of a sonic cannon could incapacitate the average citizen for hours – as soon as any citizen showed signs of recovering, Dredd ordered they be struck again, willing to use any method to stop the city tearing itself apart.

The forensics squads, when comparing Max Normal to

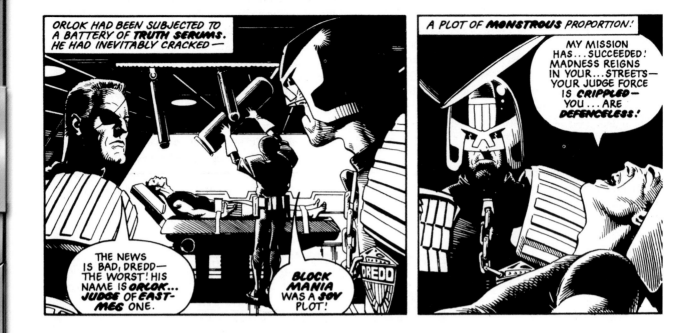

an arrested blocker had managed to discover that distortions of the brain were present in those afflicted with Block Mania. Targeting the hypothalamus, or Old Brain, Block Mania seemed to intensify the victim's natural aggression, forcing him to become surly, illogical and violent. Secondly, it stimulated his pack instinct to seek out others of his kind. The result had proven to be devastating, but the forensics squads were still no closer to finding the actual cause of the madness. No trace of any foreign substance had been found in the victim's body and water, air and sanitation supplies had all been checked for contamination. Even Psi-Div reported no psychic interference.

The northern sectors, though under constant sonic cannon bombardment, were slowly being pacified. However, the situation was about to become a lot more serious as a multi-block flare up was reported in the south of the city, in Sector 7. A missile attack launched from Fats Domino block sparked off the conflict and within minutes, several other blocks had joined battle. Every spare judge in the entire city had been pulled out to fight in the north – with minimal law enforcement present in the southern sectors, Block Mania spread faster than ever before. The few remaining judges had no choice other than to fall back but it soon became apparent that more and more of them were succumbing to Block Mania themselves. Riot foam and Stumm gas reserves were exhausted and every available sonic cannon was keeping the northern sectors

pacified. By noon the next day, Block Mania was starting to creep into the western sectors. The security of the entire city was now at stake.

The breakthrough for the Justice Department finally came when an anonymous call was placed to Judge Dredd. A citizen knew the cause of Block Mania and was willing to confess his entire involvement in exchange for judicial immunity. Unfortunately, the informant was assassinated while talking to Dredd, who was left only with a vid-trace to an apartment in Frank Zappa block. He left immediately to follow up the first and only lead to the source of Block Mania, guessing that Mega-City One was now facing a crisis that had actually been created artificially.

Frank Zappa block lay in the centre of the bitterest fighting in the entire city. For a day and a half, a fifty-block war had been raging. All alliances between the blocks had dissolved as the citizens no longer cared who they were fighting, and it was every block for itself. A well-aimed shot from neighbouring Jed Clampett block's aerial defence battery scored a devastating hit on Judge Dredd's H-Wagon as he sped towards the scene, sending the craft crashing to City Bottom. Left with no choice but to make his way through the riot-torn streets, Dredd used the speed and bike cannon of his Lawmaster to clear a path to Frank Zappa block, avoiding fleets of fighting mo-pads and maddened judges along the way. Upon arrival at the apartment within Frank Zappa where the informant had called, Judge Dredd found the murdered citizen – but more importantly he also discovered hundreds of bottles of water. The connection was obvious – despite no connection having been found by forensics squads previously, the contamination that caused Block Mania had to be in Mega-City One's water supply. Many street judges were not affected because they had used their Lawmaster's own self-contained water tank. Max Normal managed to stay immune because he had always believed water was bad for him – he was strictly a Shampagne and Clean-O-Spray man.

Alerts were immediately placed on every aqua station in the city. It was in the Atlantic Purification Plant in East Sector 29 that an intruder was soon discovered but, murdering several judges, he made his escape. By this time, the judges had withdrawn from the north, south and west sectors, to retreat to the so far unaffected central and eastern portions of Mega-City One. Despite Judge Dredd's recent discovery, forensics squads were still unable to find any contamination, so when the intruder was discovered in the purification plant handling the city's eastern water supply, orders were immediately given to capture him alive – he was obviously immune to Block Mania and his blood stream should thus contain the antidote.

Judge Giant was first on the scene and might well have managed to bring the intruder to justice were it not for a satellat, a highly sophisticated combat droid, distracting him at a critical moment during the arrest. The intruder ruthlessly killed Judge Giant and made his escape.

Having been thwarted in his attempt to contaminate the city's water supply in the central and eastern sectors, the dark intruder next targeted Weather Control Central, the huge complex that hung high above Mega-City One. Infiltrating the station, he accessed the seeding valves and caused a torrent of rain to fall upon the central and eastern sectors – a deluge contaminated with Block Mania. The intruder fled the complex in a maintenance pod and while Dredd pursued, Tek-Squads tried in vain to reverse the rain fall.

Judge Dredd finally managed to track the intruder down and arrested him, but not before his enemy had released a concentrated burst of the Block Mania contaminant in his face. An H-Wagon crew arrived to pick up the intruder and found themselves confronted by a Dredd daring them to challenge Rowdy Yates block! He was soon pacified

with a hypo injector and back in the Grand Hall of Justice, the intruder's bloodstream was analysed and the antidote identified, allowing Judge Dredd to be the first to be cured of Block Mania.

It was to be a dark day for Mega-City One, however. Tek-judges had finally stopped the contaminated rain but by now the entire city had succumbed to Block Mania. Worse still, the intruder's identity was soon revealed under interrogation and a battery of truth serums. His name was Orlock, a judge from East-Meg One on a mission to bring chaos and terror to his mortal enemies in the west. Block Mania was revealed to be a Sov plot of monstrous proportions.

Madness now reigned in the streets of Mega-City One. The Justice Department was crippled, the city defenceless. Even as Orlock was interrogated, the judges learned that East-Meg weapons were being aimed and made ready. The war to end all wars had begun; Operation Apocalypse – the death of Mega-City One!

EAST-MEG WEAPONS ARE AIMED AND READY! THE *WAR TO END ALL WARS* IS EVEN NOW BEGINNING!

Mass Combat in Judge Dredd

While the main combat rules of the d20 System are superlatively detailed for most games of Judge Dredd, they tend to become overly complicated when more than a dozen or so characters are fighting on each side in battle. To handle much larger combats, a new system is required. The mass combat system presented here will allow battles to be fought involving hundreds or even thousands of characters on each side, greatly widening the scope of any campaign. This system has much in common with the existing d20 System combat rules and players will soon find they can switch between the two quickly and easily, as and when their games dictate.

The intention of these mass combat rules, however, is not to super-detail huge sprawling mobs and their use in block wars or riots – there are hundreds of miniatures

wargames available already that do this. Instead, this system presents a realistic method of handling mass combats quickly and easily with just a few dice rolls, in order to allow the Games Master to concentrate on the actions of the true heroes in his campaign - the players.

For those players and Games Masters new to either the Judge Dredd roleplaying game or d20 System, all the tables and modifiers in this chapter may appear daunting at first. However, the basic rules are identical to those used in combat between individual characters and, once familiar with them, you will be able to resolve huge sprawling battles involving thousands of citizens with just a few dice rolls and the odd reference to the Rules Summary at the back of this book.

The Unit Roster

The Unit Roster Sheet on p64 is used to record the details and abilities of every fighting unit within an army. This sheet allows players and Games Masters alike to judge the effectiveness of any unit at a glance, and greatly aids combat resolution during mass combat.

The Unit Roster is used as a matter of convenience throughout these rules, from launching a devastating charge at an enemy across a plaza to recording casualties when being pounded by street cannon. There are many circumstances in a game where the Games Master will prefer to use standard rules from *The Player's Handbook* and the *Judge Dredd Rulebook* to resolve combat and skill checks – the Unit Roster is used only when large numbers of unit members need to perform one task at the same time.

A typical Unit Roster Sheet, detailing the crack Citi-Def of Marly Manson block, is shown overleaf;

As can be readily seen, the Unit Roster has much in common with the Creep entries of the *Judge Dredd Rulebook*, as do the unit combat rules detailed below.

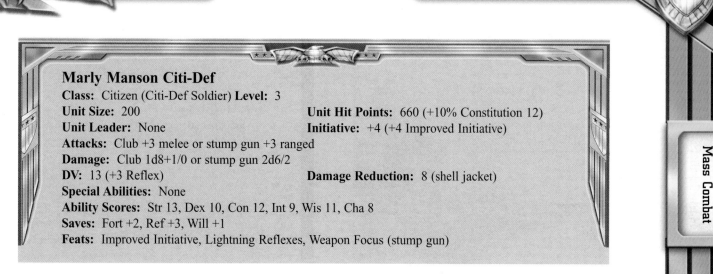

Marly Manson Citi-Def

Class: Citizen (Citi-Def Soldier) **Level:** 3

Unit Size: 200

Unit Leader: None

Attacks: Club +3 melee or stump gun +3 ranged

Damage: Club 1d8+1/0 or stump gun 2d6/2

DV: 13 (+3 Reflex)

Special Abilities: None

Ability Scores: Str 13, Dex 10, Con 12, Int 9, Wis 11, Cha 8

Saves: Fort +2, Ref +3, Will +1

Feats: Improved Initiative, Lightning Reflexes, Weapon Focus (stump gun)

Unit Hit Points: 660 (+10% Constitution 12)

Initiative: +4 (+4 Improved Initiative)

Damage Reduction: 8 (shell jacket)

Class & Level

Unit class is determined by simple majority – if a unit has 3 judges and 27 citizens, then the unit class will be noted as being citizen. The level of any unit is considered to be formed by the average of every member of the unit, rounded down – simply add up the total number of levels possessed by every character in the unit and then divide this by the number of unit members.

Prestige classes are only taken into account if the majority of a unit possesses the same prestige class. For example, if a unit of 20 judges contained 12 with the riot judge prestige class, then the class of the unit as a whole would be listed as street judge/riot judge.

Prior lives are only listed if the majority of the unit possesses the same prior life, a very rare occurrence. However, the unit of Citi-Def soldiers detailed above are one such example, and a crime lord may dispatch a unit of goons to do his dirty work.

Unit Size

This is simply a record of how many individual members are present in a unit.

Unit Hit Points

Unit Hit Points are used to measure the damage a unit may sustain in combat before being defeated or even wiped out. This is determined by simply combining the Hit Dice or character level of every unit member, modified as follows.

Majority of unit has Toughness feat	+10%
Unit has Constitution ability score modifier	+/-10% per Con modifier
Majority of unit are judges	+25%

Unit Leader

Many units are led into combat by a charismatic or bullying leader, though this is not necessary for them to be able to fight. Unit leaders are covered in more detail on p21.

Initiative

This is the Initiative modifier (calculated in the normal d20 System way, using Dexterity modifiers, etc. . .) of the majority of the unit.

Attacks, Damage & Defence Value

These are determined by simple majority – the weapons and armour the majority of the unit are armed with are assumed to be carried by all for the purposes of the Unit Roster and unit combat. The majority of the unit are also used to determine base attack bonus and any modifiers for Strength for attack and damage, and modifiers for Dexterity with respect to Defence Value.

Damage Reduction

Once again, the Damage Reduction of a unit is determined by simple majority. If, for example, 1,500 citizens in a unit of 4,000 were wearing pad armour while the rest were unarmoured, then the Damage Reduction score of the entire unit would be 0 (unarmoured).

Special Abilities

This is where any special abilities or class features possessed by the majority of the unit members are recorded.

Feats

Any unit that has a majority of members with one or more identical feats will have such feats listed on their Unit Roster. However, the following feats have no effect upon mass combat and so are never listed, no matter how many unit members possess them. However, they may still use such feats individually when not using the mass combat rules.

Alertness, Alien Anatomy, Bike Leap, Combat Reflexes, Control Crash, Data Access, Emergency Stop, Fool Birdie, Improved Bull Rush, Improved Disarm, Improved Interrogation, Improved Trip, Intuit Perp, Menacing Presence, Mobility, Nark, Quick Draw, Sixth Sense, Speed Roll, Spot Hidden Weapon, Track.

Ability Scores & Saves

The average ability scores and saves of the entire unit are noted down here on the Unit Roster.

Resolving Unit Combat

This mass combat system follows many of the rules when characters fight using the core d20 System. Unless otherwise stated below, all combat rules detailed in *The Player's Handbook* and the *Judge Dredd Rulebook* apply equally to unit combat, the Unit Roster making this transition relatively easy. Unit combat occurs whenever two units meet in battle and engage in combat. A unit must number more than 5 individuals – if a unit ever drops below this amount, these rules are no longer used and combat reverts back to that detailed in *The Player's Handbook* and the *Judge Dredd Rulebook*.

A full summary of unit combat, together with the changes required to the rules in *The Player's Handbook* and *Judge Dredd Rulebook,* is presented here.

Rounds

Unit combat is broken up into 6 second rounds, as usual.

Initiative

Before the first round of unit combat begins, each unit involved makes an Initiative check. An Initiative check is a Dexterity check (1d20 + unit's Dexterity modifier). If the unit's leader has the Leadership feat, a +2 competence bonus is applied to their Initiative check.

Attacks

Units may attack in every round they are in contact with the enemy.

Attack Roll

To score a hit that deals damage, a unit must roll the target's Defence Value or better.

Melee Attack Roll: 1d20 + base attack bonus + Strength modifier + size modifier.

Ranged Attack Roll: 1d20 + base attack bonus + Dexterity modifier + size modifier + unit size modifier + range penalty.

Large groups or mobs are far easier to hit with ranged weapons than a single character. An attacking unit will gain a bonus to its attack rolls against units based on their unit size, as detailed in the table below. Note that any attack made against a unit with a size greater than 200 will automatically hit, regardless of other modifiers, as the unit is simply too large to miss! However, the attacker will still require a line of sight, as normal.

Unit Size	Attack Roll Modifier
6-10	+1
11-20	+2
21-50	+5
51-100	+7
101-200	+9
201 or more	Automatic Hit

Damage

The majority of attacks deal damage in terms of hit points. However, units receive damage in terms of Unit Hit Points, which are effectively the number of Hit Dice or character levels of the entire unit.

Defence Value

A unit's Defence Value is the result needed for an enemy unit to successfully make an attack roll.

Defence Value: 10 + total Reflex save + size modifier.

Unit Hit Points

Unit Hit Points represent how much damage a unit can take before they are considered to be wiped out.

Attack Options

When attacking, a unit has four basic options;

Charge: A unit not engaged in melee combat may charge an enemy with this attack option.

Close Quarter Attack: A unit already involved in melee combat may make melee attacks. Units that can strike more than once each round may do so with this attack option.

FROM THE NEIGHBOURING BLOCKS, CRAZED CITIZENS POURED FORTH!

Firefight: A unit may make ranged attacks. Units that can attack more than once each round may do so with this attack option.

Withdraw: If involved in ranged or melee combat, a unit may attempt to withdraw.

Individual Unit Members

Any unit member not actively engaged in unit combat may act as normal, following all the combat rules in *The Player's Handbook* and the *Judge Dredd Rulebook*. This includes making attacks of their own, manifesting psi-talent or any other action permissible.

Movement

Units are never considered to move once involved in unit combat, due to their close proximity to one another. For more detailed combats where several units are taking part on each side, refer to the next chapter, Maps and Miniatures.

Attacks of Opportunity

Attacks of opportunity are only used in unit combat when one unit attempts to charge another unit or withdraw from combat. The act of withdrawing or charging generates an attack of opportunity.

Taking Damage

Unit Hit Points are a representation of how much damage a unit can take before they are completely slaughtered or routed. A unit reduced to 0 Unit Hit Points is considered vanquished, though members may not all be necessarily slain. Rules for determining how many survive unit combat are detailed on p22. The Games Master should periodically readjust the unit size of any unit suffering casualties.

Other Considerations

If the majority of members in a unit have a special ability (the Aura of Unease of 10th level SJS judges, for example, or a unit under the effect of a Citi-Def Officer's Inspiring Speech), then this too applies to unit combat. Bonuses to attack, damage and related rolls are easy to apply to the mass combat system.

The rules for flat-footed combatants are not used in unit combat.

In addition, the following rules from the Combat chapter of *The Player's Handbook* are never used in unit combat;

Miscellaneous Actions, Injury and Death, Flanking, Aid Another, Bull Rush, Disarm, Grapple, Mounted Combat, Overrun, Trip

The following rules from the Combat chapter of the *Judge Dredd Rulebook* are never used in unit combat;

Running Gunfights, Spraying an Area, Stray Shots, Called Shots

Charge Attack Option

A unit not currently engaged in melee combat may charge an enemy unit. In doing so, the unit gains the normal +2 charge bonus to its attack roll. However, the unit will also suffer a –2 penalty to its Defence Value for one round. The charge option is the only way in which a unit may initiate melee combat with another.

A unit being charged may make a ranged attack of opportunity against its attacker. It may not make a melee attack of opportunity.

Close Quarter Attack Option

Unit combat is treated in the same way as combats between characters in that Initiative checks are made, followed by attack and damage rolls. If a hit is scored, a damage roll is made normally with the result being deducted from the target's Unit Hit Points. There are, however, some important differences to be aware of.

Outmatching

When one unit heavily outnumbers another, they will soon find they are able to cause an excessive amount of damage upon their enemies while suffering little in return. The table below is used to grant attack, damage and morale modifiers to units who heavily outmatch their enemies, or are outmatched in return, when engaged in melee combat. Modifiers for damage rolls are only taken into account *after* any Damage Reduction for the target unit has been applied.

Firefight Attack Option

Many units are equipped with stump guns, laser rifles and other ranged weapons. The effect of an entire unit firing or hurling ranged weapons can be devastating for while citizens are not always renowned for being accurate

Unit Size is. . .	Attack Roll Modifier	Damage Roll Modifier	Morale Modifier
Ten times or more than enemy's	+5	X 10	+5
Five times enemy's	+3	X 5	+3
Three times enemy's	+2	X 3	+2
Twice enemy's	+1	X 2	+1
Less than twice but more than 50% of enemy's	+0	-	+0
50% of enemy's	-1	X 1	-1
33% of enemy's	-2	X 1	-2
20% of enemy's	-3	X 1	-3
10% or less of enemy's	-5	X ½	-5

marksmen, a hail of bullets directed into a packed enemy unit can cause utter carnage. The use of street cannon and other heavy weapons on the battlefield takes this kind of warfare to a new level – huge shells can be launched straight into the mass of an enemy unit, creating absolute terror as dozens of unit members are slain by each shot.

Firing Ranged Weapons

Ranged attacking units make a normal attack roll against their target's Defence Value, as described in the *Judge Dredd Rulebook*.

Recording Damage

If a hit is scored, a damage roll is made normally, with the result being deducted from the target's Unit Hit Points. This damage roll, however, is modified as shown below, depending on the unit size of the attackers – larger units are able to fire great numbers of missiles, causing an immense amount of damage against their enemies.

Unit Size of Attacker	Damage Modifier
6-10	-
11-20	-
21-50	-
51-100	X 2
101-200	X 3
201-500	X 4
501-1,000	X 5
1,001-2,500	X 8
2,501-5,000	X 12
5,001-10,000	X 15
10,001 or more	X 20

A minimum of 1 point of damage will always be caused, even if the dice roll is modified to 0 or less. Modifiers for damage rolls are only taken into account *after* any Damage Reduction for the target unit has been applied.

Area Effect Weapons

During the greatest riots and block wars, some truly hideous weapons may be brought to bear on densely packed units – a salvo of high-explosive missiles can bring a desperate charge to an immediate halt as multiple explosions slay hundreds of citizens within seconds. For obvious reasons, any weapon with an area of effect can have a devastating impact on unit combat.

Weapons with an area of effect will grant a damage modifier for an attacking unit, as shown on the table below. As always, this modifier to damage is only taken into account after any Damage Reduction score for the defending unit has been applied.

Area Effect	Damage Modifier
5 ft.	X 1½
10 ft.	X 4
15 ft.	X 8
20 ft.	X 10
30 ft.	X 15
60 ft.	X 20
100 ft.	X 40
Cone	Additional x2

Example of Damage

The Marly Manson Citi-Def unit, described at the start of this chapter, are attacking a unit of 200 citizens clothed in pad armour. Successfully rolling to hit, they score 8 points of damage from their stump guns. The Damage Reduction of the citizens' pad armour immediately reduces this to 4 points of damage. However, the Citi-Def get a x3 damage modifier for having 200 members in their unit (12 points of damage) and a further x1½ modifier for using stump guns, which have a 5 ft. area of effect. This gives the Citi-Def a total of 18 points of damage caused against the citizens, who are no doubt reeling from the blast.

Unit Withdraw Attack Option

A unit may choose to withdraw if the fight runs against them, either to regroup before launching another attack or to attempt to break off from combat altogether.

A unit attempting to withdraw from melee combat instead of attacking in a round immediately provokes an attack of opportunity from their enemy. This may be either a melee or ranged attack of opportunity, at the discretion of the enemy.

A unit attempting to withdraw from ranged combat instead of attacking will immediately provoke a ranged attack of opportunity from their enemy.

Once a unit withdraws, the unit combat is assumed to have ended with the withdrawing unit considered vanquished and fleeing. However, the withdrawing unit is permitted to make a Morale check (see below). If successful, it has the option of returning to the combat at any time.

Morale

There are very few units who will truly fight to the death. As the enemy swarms over barricades and defences,

long-time comrades start to fall and hails of bullets rain down, many citizens may choose to throw down their weapons rather than risk a cruel death.

Morale checks are made in unit combat whenever the circumstances listed on the table below are met. The DC required to be rolled for each circumstance is also given.

Morale Circumstance	Morale check DC
Unit Hit Points reduced to half of original score	15
Unit Hit Points reduced to one quarter of original score	10
Unit in melee combat suffers more damage in a round than enemy	15
Unit suffers a hit from an enemy of three times or greater Unit Hit Points	15
Unit withdraws from combat	20

The following modifiers apply to Morale checks;

Morale	Modifier
Unit has no leader	-4
Unit Leader	+ Leader's Charisma modifier
Morale modifier*	+/- Morale modifier
Unit Leader has Leadership feat	+ Leader's Character Level
Player actions	See p25

* Morale modifiers may come from any source, not just those listed on the outmatching table above. For example, the *demoralise* psi-power inflicts a -1 morale penalty to attack rolls – however, in unit combat, it will also inflict a penalty to Morale checks, so long as the entire unit is affected.

If a Morale check is failed, the unit automatically makes a withdraw option in its next round and will attempt to leave the battlefield at the fastest possible speed. A unit must pass a Morale check at DC 20 in order to rally and make another attack option in the following round – those failing this last Morale check will have their unit members disperse as they run for their lives. The unit is considered to be destroyed. Players are under no obligation to flee, but from this point they will be fighting on their own!

Unit Leaders

Not every unit requires a leader in order to be able to fight and, indeed, many citizen mobs do not possess any, being led forward by simplepack instinct. However, such units will lack any tactical finesse and will be utterly incapable of following orders, often acting in seemingly random patterns.

A good leader, however, will keep a tight rein on the men he leads into battle and will also provide a focal point for the unit's actions. A good leader can make all the difference between a unit standing its ground to defend an objective, or running away when the first shots are fired.

Any character can attempt to lead a unit, though it takes a truly gifted individual to lead a large number of citizens in a full scale battle. A character can lead a unit of a size no greater than twice his Charisma score.

However, characters with experience in command can lead far greater numbers. A character with the Leadership feat can lead a unit of a size up to ten times his Charisma score. Those with Advanced Leadership can lead twenty times their Charisma score. A unit leader must stay within 30 ft. of his unit at all times or else it will automatically become leaderless.

PARTICIPANTS IN BLOCK WARS ARE GRIPPED BY A FORM OF *MASS HYSTERIA*. EVEN AS THE *RIOT FOAM* SOLIDIFIES AROUND THEM, THEY FIGHT ON –

KEEP POURING IT ON!

GUESS WE NIPPED THIS ONE IN THE BUD, DREDD!

DROKK! DON'T COUNT ON IT, FLINN...!

Mass Combat

Army Leaders

Characters with Advanced Leadership are awesome figures on the battlefield, able to send large numbers of men into danger without fear of them retreating under heavy fire. However, they are also able to take a more strategic view of any battlefield and instead of leading a unit themselves, direct the leaders of several units simultaneously to complete mission objectives. In order to do this, the character must possess the Advanced Leadership feat and remain in contact with his unit leaders (usually through communicators). He may simultaneously command a number of unit leaders (and thus, their units) equal to his Charisma score. Such a character is called an army leader.

Leaderless Units

Without a leader, even squads of highly disciplined judges can lose coherency and act contrary to any mission goals. A unit without a leader will likely attack the first enemy it sees, without provocation. The Games Master takes control of any leaderless units, giving them actions and attack options as he sees fit, to reflect the unit's current mental state. Without a leader, it is likely that a unit will withdraw and disperse once it starts taking heavy casualties, something the Justice Department is all too aware of when pacifying riots.

Judges are known for their tactics of targeting the leaders of any mass disturbance first and so any citizen unit may become leaderless in a relatively short period of time. Any character allied to a leaderless unit may attempt to become its leader by making a successful Charisma check at DC 15 (+5 bonus if Leadership feat possessed). Only one character per round may attempt to do this.

Street Gangs

As a quick note, you may notice that as a character rises in level, he will find that he can no longer control the whole of his own street gang in battle. This is entirely intentional and such characters will quickly discover that they must rely on their lieutenant and other allies in order to lead their street gangs effectively against a mobilised enemy.

Recovering Casualties

Unit Hit Points do not track actual deaths amongst a unit, though there are likely to be plenty of those. Instead it demonstrates a unit's ability to continue fighting through collective death, injury and surrender.

At the end of every unit combat, whether involving ranged or melee attacks, a percentage of the lost Unit Hit Points may be automatically recovered as the injured are helped, the shirkers come out of hiding and the death toll finally totalled.

Ranged Combat: At the end of any combat involving purely ranged weapons, 50%, rounding down, of lost Unit Hit Points may be recovered.

Winning Melee Combat: At the end of any melee combat, the victor of the combat may recover 50%, rounding down, of lost Unit Hit Points.

Losing Melee Combat: At the end of any melee combat, the defeated side may recover 25%, rounding down, of lost Unit Hit Points.

These percentages are further modified as follows.

Character with at least 4 ranks in Medical skill present	+1% per character (max. +20%)
Unit withdrew from melee combat	-20%
Unit possess the Improved Recover feat	+10%

Mass Arrests

It takes a brave judge to stand in the path of a rampaging mob and order them all to surrender. Many have tried throughout the history of Mega-City One and paid the price for their foolhardy bravery. Mobs a hundred strong or more are virtually impossible to bring to a halt by direct order but some judges are able to tap into the herd instinct of smaller units and, with sufficient authority, cause them to surrender.

Normal Arrest checks are never made in unit combat and only judges with the Mass Arrest feat (see p40) are permitted to try arresting an entire unit.

To make a Mass Arrest check, a judge must roll 1d20 + his Charisma modifier + his character level. The result is the maximum unit size he can force to immediately surrender. However, he must be able to force at least half of the entire unit to surrender or automatically fail.

For example, Judge Caliber, a 7th level street judge with a Charisma score of 15, stands before a juve gang with 44 members and orders them to surrender. He rolls an 11, adding 7 for his character level and a further 2 for his Charisma modifier, for a total of 20. It is a good effort and many juves are swayed by his words, but because he did not manage to convince more than half of their number, they shake off his words and charge forward to attack.

A Mass Arrest check may be modified by the following circumstances.

Circumstance	Mass Arrest check Modifier
Every Pat-Wagon or H-Wagon in sight of unit	+2
Every Manta Prowl Tank in sight of unit	+3
Unit in cover	-5
Unit involved in combat	-2
Unit already faced Mass Arrest check	-5
Judge has 10 or more ranks in Intimidate	+2
Unit reduced to half original unit hit points or less	+2

Judges will likely face additional problems, even if they do convince large numbers of citizens to surrender. If unable to capture or chain them to holding posts within a few minutes, it is highly likely small groups will begin to sneak away, risking a resisting arrest charge in order to keep their freedom – street judges tackling riots and rumbles are advised to make sure they have adequate back-up before risking their lives by arresting entire mobs.

Commandos

Any unit wearing armour with no higher Damage Reduction than 6 may be designated as a commando unit, taking to the field in a small dispersed formation that allows them to operate with great flexibility. A commando unit only suffers half damage from any ranged attack and gains a +2 competence bonus on all Initiative checks. However, no commando unit may have more than 20 members at any one time.

Vehicles

Upon the battlefield, a unit leader may find himself facing an enemy force comprising of far more than mere citizens or judges. Arrayed against his own unit may be dreaded Pat-Wagons, armoured truks and awesome Manta Prowl Tanks. These vehicles can dominate any battlefield with their firepower and sheer durability.

Vehicles are treated as if each were a unit in its own right. However, to reflect their increased capabilities, vehicles have a slightly different profile to regular units as well as some special rules which give them the capability to crush entire mobs with their great weaponry.

The Vehicle Roster

The Vehicle Roster Sheet on p64 is used to record the details and abilities of every vehicle within this mass combat system. This sheet allows players and Games Masters alike to judge the effectiveness of any vehicle at a glance, and greatly aids mass combat resolution within games.

A typical Vehicle Roster Sheet, detailing a Manta Prowl Tank, is shown below;

As can be readily seen, the Vehicle Roster has much in common with the Unit Roster detailed earlier.

The attacks score is simply a list of the weapons mounted on the vehicle, together with the ranged attack bonus and fire control of the crewman of each.

Vehicles in Battle

In most respects, vehicles are handled in the same way as any other unit. However, there are some exceptions within unit combat that reflects their ponderous nature upon the battlefield.

† All vehicles suffer a –4 circumstance penalty to their Initiative checks.

† Every vehicle is considered to be a separate unit – they are never combined to form larger units.

† Vehicles are considered to automatically pass any Morale check they are called upon to make.

† All vehicles are considered to have their own leader.

† No vehicle can ever make an attack of opportunity.

Players in Unit Combat

The centre of action for any roleplaying scenario are the players themselves and, in unit combat, they truly have the opportunity to act as heroes. As a unit crashes into the enemy, the players will lead their men forward, all the while seeking to engage opposing unit leaders, destroy enemy vehicles and save their allies from a torrent of firepower.

The rules presented in this chapter are designed to allow the easy integration of players into unit combat, with as little work as possible required on the part of the Games Master. The length of a combat round, be it featuring the actions of characters or an entire unit is always six seconds. Thus, whatever a character could normally attempt in a normal combat round will apply equally in unit combat.

Unit Combats

Player characters are never counted as part of the unit when calculating the Unit Roster – they always act independently, even if they are mere foot soldiers, thus allowing them to do all sorts of heroic (or cowardly) things. Under normal circumstances, combat for player characters in melee combat is handled in exactly the same way as presented in *The Player's Handbook* and the *Judge Dredd Rulebook*. They are, however, permitted to attack enemy units directly.

If two units are in combat with one another, players may choose to aid one side. To do so, they engage in combat with one or more members of the enemy unit, using the normal combat rules presented in *The Player's Handbook* and the *Judge Dredd Rulebook*. Everyone involved in the

Vehicle: Manta Prowl Tank TV/IIX
Hit Points: 450
Attacks: Peterson High Intensity Laser Cannon +8, 2 twin-linked Anti-Personnel Laser Cannon +8, 4 Stumm Gas Dispensers +8, Riot Foam Jets +8
Damage: Peterson High Intensity Laser Cannon 4d12/20, 2 twin-linked Anti-Personnel Laser Cannon 4d8/14, 4 Stumm Gas Dispensers, Riot Foam Jets
DV: 2
Damage Reduction: 20

combat acts in Initiative order, so the player characters may have the chance to act before anyone else. However, if they manage to slay or subdue any of their enemies, then the Hit Dice or character level of the enemies they overcome is immediately deducted from the Unit Hit Point score.

For example, whilst leading his fellow judges to attack the renegade Marly Manson Citi-Def in a desperate charge, Judge Humpy, rolling the highest initiative of the combat, attacks a Citi-Def Officer as his men engage the rest of the enemy. The Unit Hit Point score of the Citi-Def is 660. Judge Humpy dispatches his officer foe in one round of combat – the officer was an 8th level character (having 6 levels as a citizen and 2 levels as a Citi-Def Officer), and thus the Citi-Def lose 8 Unit Hit Points immediately, bringing them down to a total of 652. The units now fight as described in this chapter, in remaining initiative order.

Players take damage from unit attacks as normal – however, units will always use damage modifiers based on their unit size, making large numbers of citizens potentially lethal, even for high level judges.

For example, the battle has not gone well for Judge Humpy and his unit has run away. Foolishly, he decides to stay and fight against the 400 surviving Citi-Def soldiers left after the last round of combat. Consulting the outmatching table, he is outnumbered by more than ten to one and so the Citi-Def gain a +5 bonus to their attack rolls and multiply all damage by ten. Even though they are only using the butts of their guns as clubs, Judge Humpy is in a lot of trouble. Unsurprisingly, they succeed in their attack roll and roll for damage – clubs do 1d8 points of damage, with a +1 bonus for the Citi-Def's Strength of 13. 6 points of damage is scored, but this is multiplied by 10 because the unit outmatches Judge Humpy. His body suit armour's Damage Reduction of 6 still comes into effect, but 54 points of damage are still scored. Judge Humpy is left as nothing more than a stain on the Tweenblock Plaza and the Marly Manson Citi-Def are free to continue their reign of terror in Mega-City One.

Unit Morale

Players are immune to the effects of unit morale, as detailed on p20, though unit members are likely to take a dim view of players who continue to fight as they try to surrender. However, many of a player's actions in combat may have a direct influence on how their unit fights. The table below lists some of the more common actions a player may attempt to boost the morale of his unit, though the Games Master is welcome to add others as the need arises – in essence, a player should always be rewarded for bravery and will certainly earn the respect of the unit. Those who act in a cowardly manner will likely detract from the morale of their unit. The morale bonus earned applies to the unit's attack and damage rolls for the rest of the combat, as well as to standard Morale checks, as detailed on p21.

Player Action	Morale Bonus to Unit
Slaying enemy unit leader	+2
Destroying enemy vehicle	+3
Fleeing battle	-4
Slaying 10% or more of enemy unit in one attack	+1

Non-Player Characters

It is strongly recommended that these rules for players also be adopted for important non-player characters, be they allied to the party or enemies. In this way, even a lowly juve gang should not have its punk leader subsumed into the Unit Roster – he will act as an independent character, encouraging his unit and attacking the players at their weakest points, even earning the morale bonuses presented above.

Full-Scale Battle

The unit combat rules presented in this chapter will allow players to lead a group of fighting men in riots and rumbles. However, this mass combat system is capable of reflecting much larger battles, such as block wars, where multiple units on each side engage in a desperate fight to claim victory.

See the next chapter for rules on commanding larger forces.

Maps and Miniatures

So far, we have looked at large street battles involving one unit on each side. However, a great deal of fun may be had once multiple units and even multiple forces begin engaging in the same battle. The Games Master is free to conduct such scenarios in a narrative style, merely using the mass combat rules whenever two units in the game actually meet. Others, however, will wish to use maps and even miniatures in order to demonstrate to their players exactly what is happening in the game, and so grant an added tactical edge to their scenarios – once players can see exactly where enemy units are, they will gain a great deal of enjoyment in outwitting their foes by performing flanking manoeuvres, scouting operations and then leading direct assaults on enemy-held positions.

This chapter takes a look at ways Games Masters can introduce such complexities into their scenarios. It should always be borne in mind, however, that Judge Dredd is a roleplaying game, not a wargame or tactical simulation. What we should primarily concentrate upon are the actions of the players and how they affect the world around them, not super-detailing every Citi-Def or judge unit they may battle against. The whole point of mass combat in Judge Dredd is to quickly resolve the actions of potentially thousands of combatants with just a few dice rolls in order to bring the focus back to the players as quickly as possible. Follow these guidelines, don't get caught up in the complexities of controlling hundreds of units and you will not go far wrong the next time you decide what your campaign really requires is a seriously *big* block war. . .

Creating Maps

An example map of the Tweenblock Plaza separating Madonna Ciccone and the Cher High Rise is featured below. As will become readily apparent, a Games Master need not go into too much detail when creating such maps, for they are designed to depict the tactical situation on a suitably large scale.

The standard scale for maps in d20 System games is 1 inch to 5ft. However, it is recommended that for the purposes of mass combat, Games Masters use an overlaid one-inch grid on their maps, with a scale of 1 inch to 100 ft. This scale makes it easy to keep track of the range increments of most weapons used in the Judge Dredd roleplaying game, as well as the positions of large units – 400 human-sized characters will fill one square. For easy reference, the table below demonstrates how many squares units of varying sizes will fill at this scale.

Unit Size	No. of Squares Covered
400	1
800	2
1,200	3
2,000	5
4,000	10
8,000	20
20,000	50
40,000	100
100,000	250
250,000	625

Units large enough to cover multiple squares on maps can take any shape, so long as each square covered by the unit is adjacent to another occupied by it.

Maps may be of any size and Games Masters may soon find themselves sketching plans on huge sheets of graph paper in order to accommodate their latest riot or block war! However, a Games Master may also adjust the scale of his maps as he sees fit – this will have no effect on the mass combat system rules, only on the number of squares each unit takes up, range increments for weapons and movement. A particularly large clash, for example, may require the Games Master to increase the scale of his maps up to 1 inch to 1,000 ft. – at this scale, every square will hold 40,000 human-sized characters!

Movement

Games Masters will find it convenient to round up 'odd' measurements when using maps in the mass combat system, particularly with regards to movement. The average human has a base speed of 30 ft. per round, and so will take some time to move even one space on a 1 inch to 100 ft. scale map. The easy solution is to simply require characters to take three rounds to move one square on the map – even though they are only moving a total of 90 ft., the 'odd' 10 ft. can be safely ignored at this scale. Characters or units running (four times their base speed) will actually cover 120 ft. However, on mass combat maps, the Games Master can safely round this down to 100 ft. and thus move them one square each round.

The Games Master, will always be the final arbitrator of whether any given character or unit can cover a set distance over any particular period of time.

The basic vehicle rules in the *Judge Dredd Rulebook* list a conversion table so those travelling at crawling speed can easily interact with characters on foot. However, when using maps in this mass combat system, the full speed of vehicles can be fully realised. Below is a simple conversion table to provide a quick reference for a vehicle's speed in mph, adjusted for feet per round and squares per round. The Games Master can easily alter the latter to suit whatever scale of map he is currently using.

Vehicle Speed	Ft. per Round	Squares per Round
25 mph	220 ft.	2
50 mph	440 ft.	4
75 mph	660 ft.	7
100 mph	880 ft.	9
125 mph	1,100 ft.	11
150 mph	1,320 ft.	13
175 mph	1,540 ft.	15
200 mph	1,760 ft.	18
225 mph	1,980 ft.	20
250 mph	2,200 ft.	22
275 mph	2,420 ft.	24
300 mph	2,640 ft.	26
325 mph	2,860 ft.	29
350 mph	3,080 ft.	31
375 mph	3,300 ft.	33
400 mph	3,520 ft.	35
425 mph	3,740 ft.	37
450 mph	3,960 ft.	40
475 mph	4,180 ft.	42
500 mph	4,400 ft.	44

Using Miniatures

Many players have a passion for using miniatures in their games. As well as providing the best way to readily understand any combat or tactical situation, there is just something nice about a set of well-painted miniatures gracing the tabletop alongside appropriate scenery. However, even the most dedicated painter is likely to balk at the idea of painting enough citizens to take part in a block war scenario.

Fortunately, this mass combat system comes to the ready rescue – by using a one inch grid on your maps, you will find that most commercially available miniatures can be used to represent one square of a unit. A group of 1,200 judges called in to deal with a multiple block war, for example, would cover three adjacent squares and thus could be represented by three judge miniatures. A large unit of 4,800 citizens is easily represented by 12 citizen miniatures placed on adjacent squares.

Those without miniatures may still use maps in this way, but with counters or cards used in place of individual miniatures. Games Masters with access to a photocopier may even wish to make multiple copies of their maps and actually draw or sketch out the positions of units round by round. Any of these methods are acceptable when using the mass combat system detailed in *The Rookie's Guide to Block Wars*. What is important is that both the players and the Games Master know what is happening in the scenario at all times.

BLOCK WARS WERE NOTHING NEW TO MEGA-CITY ONE. THE BOREDOM AND CLAUS-TROPHOBIC OVERCROWDING OF FUTURE LIVING BROUGHT TENSIONS TO A KNIFE-EDGE. INTER-BLOCK VIOLENCE COULD ERUPT AT ANY TIME –

Cityblocks

The great towering cityblocks of Mega-City One are at the centre of most civil disturbances. Citizens feel a natural loyalty towards their own block, where they will spend the majority of their lives. When roused to anger, they readily join with others they can easily identify with – in Mega-City One, this will almost always be the fellow residents of their own block.

Each cityblock, from the sky-rises that rise over a mile above city bottom to the smallest of con-apts, is engineered to last, providing suitable accommodation for perhaps thousands upon thousands of citizens and their families. Though riots may rage all around these mighty buildings, they are rarely damaged much beyond heavy vandalism and stand rigid even as their inhabitants make war. The sight of a cityblock actually collapsing under the punishment of a block war is not one a citizen can ever expect to see in his life – but it has been known to happen.

Creating Cityblocks

The Games Master is free to create any cityblock he chooses to include in his scenarios, regardless of dimensions and population. Mega-City One is a gigantic city and, at some point, almost any conceivable building is likely to have been constructed. However, in this chapter we provide a ready to use system for quickly generating cityblocks, to aid a Games Master in populating his sector and give some guideline on how such buildings should actually look and function.

There are six main cityblock types in Mega-City One;

Cityblock: This is the standard block being constructed in Mega-City One in 2124 and is by far the most common. Though varying wildly in individual design, these blocks are all very similar to one another in terms of size and capacity, and have been a feature of the city since the end of the Apocalypse War.

Low Rise: These are very small blocks, often confused with con-apts. However, being characteristically much thinner, low rises tend to be take up far less space in the city and are usually far below the luxury standards of a con-apt.

Con-Apt: Con-apts were originally designed to provide a slightly more luxurious existence for those citizens able

ORIEN SPECK'S BLOCK, *FRANK ZAPPA*, LAY IN THE CENTRE OF THE BITTEREST FIGHTING. FOR A DAY AND A HALF A *FIFTY-BLOCK WAR* HAD BEEN RAGING.

NOW, NO BLOCK KNEW WHOSE SIDE THEY WERE ON—AND NO BLOCK CARED!

ALL GUNS FIRE AT WILL!

to afford it though many are now in an advanced state of disrepair and are being demolished in favour of the far more efficient cityblocks. Many still exist in the city though and their citizens tend to be extremely loyal to their home, perhaps because they are so greatly outnumbered in any block war.

Pre-Atomic: These are among the oldest blocks to be found anywhere within Mega-City One and few remain in their original condition. The first true cityblocks to be built anywhere in the world, most are all but falling down from a lack of maintenance and, though they have survived the rigours of several wars, the Housing Department is anxious to replace them with more modern designs as quickly as possible.

Slum: Slum blocks are usually pre-atomic designs that have had virtually no maintenance throughout their existence, though some older cityblocks also fall into this category. The Housing Department intentionally places the very worst elements of society in such blocks in order to contain them and stop them mixing with ordinary, decent citizens. The result is a block where crime rates soar and inhabitants seem to work collectively to destroy their own home, piece by piece. Few slum blocks are allowed to stand for more than a few years but city officials are often extremely reluctant to give the go ahead for demolition as this just means the inhabitants have to be housed elsewhere.

Luxy-Block: These are the pinnacle of Mega-City One architects' achievements. Soaring into the sky, they provide every luxury a citizen could hope for and contain a fair army of robots dedicated to fulfilling the needs of the inhabitants. All this comes at a tremendous cost, however, and most luxy-blocks have many empty apartments, for not many citizens in the city have the credits to spare. Though this leads to increased rates for the inhabitants that remain, they are typically the sort of citizens who willingly pay more for solitude and peace.

There are, of course, many other different blocks constructed all over the city, such as crock blocks and problem blocks, but they are all based on the designs listed above. The Games Master is free to change the designation of any block detailed here to suit the purposes of his own scenarios.

All blocks in Mega-City One can be detailed in just a few lines as the example below shows;

Dredd's Comportment

'Part of a judge's training is to be calm and behave with dignity at all times.'

On Behaviour

Callista Flockhart Block
Sector 190, MegWest
Built: 2119
Type: Cityblock
Levels: 194
Population: 67,900
Citi-Def: 800, 2nd level
Damage Reduction: 18
Structural Hit Points: 38,800

In most ways, the Callista Flockhart block of Sector 190 is fairly average when compared to other such buildings in the city.

The first three lines of this block simply list a few background details created by the Games Master – the block's name, where it is based in the city and when it was built. Almost all cityblocks in Mega-City One are named after famous personalities (real or fictional) over the past three centuries, providing the Games Master with an endless source of inspiration – all you need do is open a newspaper, watch the television or pick up a book on 20th century history to find an inexhaustible source of cityblock names. A few examples are presented below.

Sly Stallone Block, Cruise and Kidman Twin Rises, Michael Hunt Crock Block, Dan Tanna Block, Ant Dilly Con-Apt, T&J Hooker Low Rise, Dicky Wilson Luxy, Fat Bloke Big Block, Carl Sagan Block, Tolkeen Con-Apt, Kylie Minogue Block, Buddy Holly Block, John Prezza Block, Dom Preston Luxy

The type of block is chosen by the Games Master, based on what he needs for his scenario and the rest is randomly generated using the table below.

Cityblock Creation

	City Block	Low Rise	Con-Apt	Pre-Atomic Block	Slum Block	Luxy-Block
Levels	1d100 + 150	1d120 + 12	1d20 + 30*	1d100 + 100	1d100 + 100	1d100 + 150
Population	2d6 x 50 per level	2d6 x 10 per level	2d6 x 25 per level	1d6 x 50 per level	2d6 x 50 per level	1d6 x 25 per level
Citi-Def Size	1d20 x 100	-	1d10 x 50	1d10 x 100	1d20 x 200	1d6 x 50
Citi-Def Level	1d4	-	1d3	1d2	1d2	1d3 + 1
Damage Reduction	1d3 + 16	1d3 + 14	1d3 + 16	1d3 + 14	1d3 + 14	1d3 + 16
Structural Hit Points	200 per level	100 per level	125 per level	150 per level	150 per level	200 per level

* Con-apts can actually be as low as three levels in height and some are over fifty. Such buildings are very rare though and left to the discretion of the Games Master.

Levels: This is simply an indication of how many levels (storeys) the block towers into the sky. It is also used to help determine the population and structural hit points of the block.

Population: This lists the maximum capacity the block can comfortably house. Due to the housing shortage in Mega-City One, few blocks will house anything less than their maximum capacity. Simply multiply the number generated in the table above by the number of levels the block has to find out its total population capacity.

Citi-Def Size: This is the number of permanent members the block has in its Citi-Def unit and is equal to Unit Size should they ever use the mass combat system detailed in Chapter 3.

Citi-Def Level: This reflects the competency of the Citi-Def unit (and is usually not very high!). The average member of the Citi-Def can be presumed to be a citizen of this level and have the Citi-Def Soldier prior life. Sample Citi-Def soldiers may be found at the end of this chapter.

Damage Reduction: As detailed in the *Judge Dredd Rulebook*, this gives the relative armour of the block and its ability to simply shrug off incoming attacks.

Structural Hit Points: Even the smallest block is a massive construction, comprising millions of tons of plascrete, rockcrete, plastisteel and other materials. They are extremely difficult for ordinary weapons to even damage, let alone destroy. The use of structural hit points in games of Judge Dredd is detailed below.

Block Facilities

It is claimed that the cityblocks of Mega-City One contain everything a citizen needs throughout his entire life and, in theory, he need never leave the block from birth to death. Few citizens take this extreme but each block contains far more than mere apartments. It can be assumed that every block has plenty of shopping malls, schools, libraries, med centres, hoverports, parks and other facilities to fully accommodate its citizens. Even slum blocks will have these features though they will likely be dilapidated and out-of-date, if they are functional at all.

Attacking Cityblocks

Even the lowest punk on the streets knows that if you wish to have a serious chance of bringing an entire cityblock down, you need some major ordnance on your side. Even high-powered lasers and explosive shells may do little to chip away at the towering buildings. When one block attacks another, it is going to need a great deal of both planning and firepower if it is to succeed in its ultimate aim of actually destroying its enemy, rather than just fighting with its citizens.

Comparatively speaking, it is fairly easy to blow holes in apartment walls and shopping malls, using the Attack an

Object rules on page 78 of the *Judge Dredd Rulebook*. However, this will have little to no effect upon the structural integrity of the block itself. To actually destroy a block and bring it crashing down to city bottom in a pile of rubble requires an altogether different approach.

Structural Hit Points

Every cityblock detailed in these rules has a number of structural hit points, likely numbering several thousand. Each structural hit point of a cityblock is equal to ten hit points of a character or vehicle.

Any attack launched at a cityblock will automatically hit, with no need for an attack roll. These buildings are so large that even a cross-eyed punk will have trouble missing one. However, an attack by a weapon must cause ten full hit points worth of damage in order to deal one structural hit point of damage to a cityblock, after Damage Reduction has been taken into account. Any lesser amount is ignored and disregarded, with the attack simply bouncing off the side of the cityblock.

For example, two members of the Marly Manson Citi-Def have managed to acquire missile launchers during a block war and are now firing salvoes directly into Callista Flockhart Block. Even though two missiles have hit the block and have a high enough Armour Piercing score to ignore its Damage Reduction, they are not having an easy time of it. The first hi-ex missile deals 9 points of damage – not a good shot against any target but upon a cityblock this is not enough to knock off a single structural hit point and is simply ignored. The second missile deals 32 points of damage and so 3 structural hit points are deducted from the block, with the 'spare' 2 hit points being ignored and discarded. As the Marly Manson Citi-Def quickly learn, it is going to take a lot of ammunition to bring down Callista Flockhart. . .

Some very powerful attacks are capable of ignoring this rule and instead deal damage directly to the structural hit points of a block as if they were normal hit points. Such attacks are listed below.

† Attacks on the foundations of a block – note that such attacks must be able to directly target the core foundations of the block, usually placing the attacker right under the block itself!

† Attacks from disintegrators – a light disintegrator will deal 1d6 points of structural hit point damage with each attack, while a heavy duty disintegrator will deal 3d6 points.

† Attacks by any sonic-based weapon (such as the sonic blaster and sonic cannon). The sonic blaster will do 1d10 points of damage to a block's structural hit points

per round, without requiring an attack roll and ignoring any Damage Reduction. The sonic cannon will do 2d10 points of damage per round.

† Attacks made by units. In close quarter attacks, units attacking a cityblock always count as being less than twice but more than 50% of their enemy's unit size on the Overmatching table and so are granted no bonus. If they attack using the firefight option (which can also, of course, be used while they are actually inside the block), then the normal ranged damage modifiers table is used.

These attacks, while extremely powerful and able to shake the largest block in the city, are still subject to Damage Reduction in the normal way – a mob armed with clubs is going to be able to do nothing to affect a cityblock structurally, no matter how much vandalism they cause, but ten thousand citizens all armed with hi-explosives can pose a serious threat.

For example, the two Citi-Def soldiers of Marly Manson are joined by a mob of citizens, also armed with newly stolen missile launchers. Their unit size is now 1,000, earning them a x5 modifier to all attacks they cause with ranged weapons. Automatically hitting Callista Flockhart Block, their hi-ex missiles once more ignore the Damage Reduction score. A score of 26 is rolled for damage,

multiplied by 5 for the unit size to result in 130 points of damage. However, because they are firing as a unit, 130 is deducted straight from Callista Flockhart Block's structural hit points, rather than being treated as normal hit points.

Structural Integrity

When a cityblock has been reduced to 0 structural hit points, it is considered to have been turned into rubble and immediately collapses, as detailed below. However, it is possible to do such a terrific amount of damage to a block that it is shaken to its very foundations. One significant impact may be enough to bring a block crashing down, regardless of how many structural hit points it has. This can be even more difficult than pounding a block to rubble but a single, well-executed attack may save an aggressor a great deal of effort, if not time.

If a block ever takes more than 500 points of damage from a single attack, it must make a Structural Integrity check at DC 22. This is done by rolling 1d20 and adding the block's Damage Reduction score as a positive modifier.

If the Structural Integrity check succeeds, then the block loses structural hit points as normal from the attack but otherwise remains standing. If this check is failed, then the block – and everyone within it – is in very serious trouble, as a critical part of the building's structure has been destroyed in the attack and the entire block begins to shudder under its own weight. The cityblock will automatically collapse within 1d6 hours of the attack. Nothing can prevent this – even the finest Justice Department emergency services are incapable of stopping the fall of millions of tons of plascrete.

The 500 points of damage that must be dealt in order to force a Structural Integrity check must come from a single attack roll and may not be totalled from several, separate, attacks.

Collapsing Blocks

There are few sights more awe-inspiring than that of a cityblock crashing down to City Bottom. For the unfortunate citizens trapped within the block or present within

the surrounding area, however, it can be a positively lethal experience.

Any character inside or within 300 ft. of a collapsing block must make a Fortitude save at DC 25 or be instantly crushed to death by the rubble. In addition, they will automatically be trapped and unable to escape without outside help (normally provided within 1d3 days by Justice Department emergency teams). There is no way to avoid this fate – not even the greatest hero is fast enough to be able to 'dodge' this level of destruction! Any vehicles inside the block or within 300 ft. will automatically be destroyed.

At the Games Master's option, nearby blocks may also succumb to the destruction of their neighbours – the massive weight of a falling block may trigger the collapse of their own foundations or the entire City Bottom may be so weakened that both fall through to the Undercity. Smaller blocks may simply be buried under the rubble of a much taller neighbour. Any block the Games Master deems to be sufficiently close to a collapsing block must make a Structural Integrity check at DC 20 or also collapse, with all the effects described above.

Sample Citi-Def Soldiers

The following Citi-Def personnel are provided for Games Masters to avoid the need of constantly creating new characters and units in the middle of a game. Games Masters are also welcome to use these characters as a base for their own Citi-Def characters, altering levels, feats and skills to come up with some truly unique and memorable personalities.

Citi-Def Recruit

Citizen 1 (Citi-Def soldier); HD 1d6+3 (9); Init +1 (+1 Dex); Spd 30 ft.; DV 11 (+1 Reflex); Attack +0 club (1d8/0), or +1 stump gun (2d6/2); Fort +0, Ref +1, Will -1; Str 10, Dex 12, Con 11, Int 10, Wis 9, Cha 11.
Skills and feats: Balance +4, Climb +4, Concentration +3, Drive +5, Jump +4, Listen +4, Medical +3, Search +3, Streetwise +4, Spot +4; Endurance, Toughness.
Possessions: Club, stump gun.

Citi-Def Soldier

Citizen 2 (Citi-Def soldier); HD 2d6+3 (12); Init +1 (+1 Dex); Spd 30 ft.; DV 11 (+1 Reflex); Attack +1 knife (1d6/2), or +2 stump gun (2d6/2); Fort +0, Ref +1, Will -1; Str 10, Dex 12, Con 11, Int 10, Wis 9, Cha 11.
Skills and feats: Balance +4, Climb +4, Computer Use +2, Concentration +5, Drive +5, Jump +5, Listen +4, Medical +3, Search +4, Streetwise +5, Spot +4;

Endurance, Toughness.
Possessions: Knife, shell jacket (DR 8), stump gun.

Veteran Citi-Def Soldier

Citizen 3 (Citi-Def soldier); HD 3d6+3 (16); Init +1 (+1 Dex); Spd 30 ft.; DV 12 (+2 Reflex); Attack +2 knife (1d6/2), or +4 spit gun (2d6/6); Fort +1, Ref +2, Will +0; Str 10, Dex 12, Con 11, Int 10, Wis 9, Cha 11.
Skills and feats: Balance +4, Climb +6, Computer Use +3, Concentration +5, Drive +5, Intimidate +5, Jump +6, Listen +4, Medical +3, Search +4, Streetwise +5, Spot +5; Endurance, Toughness, Weapon Focus (spit gun).
Possessions: Knife, shell jacket (DR 8), spit gun.

Elite Citi-Def Soldier

Citizen 4 (Citi-Def soldier); HD 4d6+7 (23); Init +1 (+1 Dex); Spd 30 ft.; DV 12 (+2 Reflex); Attack +3 las-knife (1d6/10), or +5 laser rifle (4d8/14); Fort +2, Ref +2, Will +0; Str 10, Dex 12, Con 12, Int 10, Wis 9, Cha 11.
Skills and feats: Balance +4, Climb +6, Computer Use +5, Concentration +6, Drive +5, Hide +8, Intimidate +5, Jump +6, Listen +4, Medical +3, Search +4, Streetwise +5, Spot +5; Endurance, Toughness, Weapon Focus (laser rifle).
Possessions: Las-knife, laser rifle, shell jacket (DR 8).

Citi-Def Jaeger Squad Commando

Jaeger squad commando 1/citizen 7 (Citi-Def soldier); HD 1d10+7d6+11 (43); Init +1 (+1 Dex); Spd 30 ft.; DV 13 (+3 Reflex); Attack +6 las-knife (1d6/10), or +8 laser rifle (4d8/14); Fort +5, Ref +3, Will +1; Str 10, Dex 13, Con 12, Int 10, Wis 9, Cha 11.
Skills and feats: Balance +6, Climb +9, Concentration +10, Drive +7, Hide +11, Jump +8, Knowledge (military) +6, Listen +6, Medical +5, Move Silently +11, Search +5, Streetwise +5, Spot +7, Technical +6; Combat Reflexes, Endurance, Toughness, Weapon Focus (laser rifle).
Possessions: 4 hand bombs, hi-ex pack, las-knife, laser rifle, shell jacket (DR 8).

Citi-Def Officer

Citi-Def officer 2/citizen 6 (Citi-Def soldier); HD 2d8+6d6 (31); Init +1 (+1 Dex); Spd 30 ft.; DV 15 (+5 Reflex); Attack +6 las-knife (1d6/10), or +8 laser pistol (4d6/14); Fort +4, Ref +5, Will +2; Str 10, Dex 13, Con 11, Int 10, Wis 10, Cha 12.
Skills and feats: Climb +8, Drive +11, Intimidate +11, Jump +10, Knowledge (military) +11, Medical +10, Streetwise +10, Spot +11, Technical +10; Leadership, Lightning Reflexes, Skill Focus (intimidate), Weapon Focus (laser pistol).
Possessions: Las-knife, laser pistol, shell jacket (DR 8).

Characters in Block Wars

It is claimed by some Citi-Def units that it takes a special sort of soldier to thrive and survive in the midst of a block war. However, a judge will tell you any dumbo can start a civil disturbance. This chapter takes a look at the kind of characters that can get mixed up in rumbles, riots and block wars. Here you will find new prestige classes (including the infamous and highly specialised riot squad judge) and new feats that will allow characters to take full advantage of the mass combat rules presented in *The Rookie's Guide to Block Wars*, as well as make them potent adversaries in day-to-day life on the streets. Whether you are seeking to pacify large, rampaging crowds as a judge or looking to spark off the greatest battle since Block Mania, there is something for every character here!

The Riot Squad Judge

Stern, unyielding and covered in heavy-weight armour, the riot squad judge is the faceless trooper many citizens will meet if they are unfortunate enough to get caught up in a major civil disturbance. Trained to handle large mobs, the judges of the riot squads operate in small teams and yet are both taught and equipped to engage many times their own number on an equal footing. Equipped with the very best riot gear the Justice Department can provide, these judges seek to contain, pacify and arrest unruly citizens, only sweeping in to break heads when there are few other options.

Hit Die: d12.

Requirements
To qualify to become a riot squad judge, a street judge must fulfil all the following criteria.

Base Attack Bonus: +5.
Skills: Intimidate 8 ranks, Streetwise 8 ranks.
Feats: Improved Arrest, Iron Will, Nerves of Steel, Skill Focus (intimidate).

Class Skills
The riot squad judge's class skills (and the key ability for each skill) are Balance (Dex), Climb (Str), Drive (Dex), Jump (Str), Knowledge (law) (Int), Listen (Wis), Medical (Wis), Ride (Dex), Search (Int), Spot (Wis), and Streetwise (Wis).

Skill points at each level: 4 + Int modifier.

Class Features
All of the following are class features of the riot squad judge prestige class.

Specialist Equipment: In addition to a new uniform, riot squad judges are also granted riot armour, a riot shield and riot foam (no reload) to supplement their standard issue equipment. They also wear their daysticks on their belts, rather than stowing them in their Lawmasters.

Breaking Heads: Riot squad judges are highly skilled in the use of their primary crowd-dispersal weapon, the humble daystick. In their hands it can become, quite literally, a lethal weapon. Before making any attack roll with his daystick, a riot squad judge can opt to cause actual rather than subdual damage. In addition, for this attack, the daystick will have an Armour Piercing score of 4.

Shield Rush: At 2nd level, the riot squad judge learns to use his riot shield as an offensive weapon during charges, tucking himself behind it as he bears down on a crowd. When charging, the riot squad judge will not suffer the –2 charge penalty to his Defensive Value. In addition, he receives a free attack with his riot shield, at his lowest base attack bonus. This attack deals 1d8 points of damage, plus his Strength modifier, with an Armour Piercing score of 0. He does not lose his Damage Reduction bonus from his shield while attempting a Shield Rush.

Dredd's Comportment

'When a judge gets too valuable to risk, he is no longer a judge.'

On Sacrifice

The Riot Squad Judge

Level	Base Attack Bonus	Fort Save	Ref Save	Will Save	Special
1	+1	+2	+2	+2	Breaking Heads
2	+2	+3	+3	+3	Shield Rush
3	+3	+3	+3	+3	Bonus Feat
4	+4	+4	+4	+4	Defeat the Odds
5	+5	+4	+4	+4	Unit Discipline +2
6	+6/+1	+5	+5	+5	Bonus Feat
7	+7/+2	+5	+5	+5	Defensive Shield
8	+8/+3	+6	+6	+6	Counter Charge
9	+9/+4	+6	+6	+6	Bonus Feat
10	+10/+5	+7	+7	+7	Unit Discipline +4

Bonus Feat: Though highly specialised, riot squad judges train hard for life on the streets, for they often have to bear the brunt of the citizens' rage and frustration. At 3rd, 6th and 9th level, the riot squad judge receives a bonus General or Judge feat of his choice from the following list, in addition to feats gained every three levels as normal – Combat Reflexes, Dodge, Endurance, Great Fortitude, Improved Bull Rush, Improved Mass Arrest, Improved Recovery, Mass Arrest and Sixth Sense. He must meet all prerequisites for the bonus feat as usual.

Defeat the Odds: Judges of the riot squad are well used to facing mobs of far greater size than their own unit. At 4th level, any attacker of a unit led by the riot squad judge will count as being of one size class less on the Outmatching Table. A unit three times the size of that being led by the riot squad judge, for example, will count as only being twice the size.

Unit Discipline: At 5th and 10th level, the riot squad judge learns advanced unit coherency tactics that ensure any unit he leads will be resolute in combat, no matter what odds they face. When making any Morale checks as a unit leader, the riot squad judge receives the competence bonus listed on the table below.

Defensive Shield: On reaching 7th level, riot squad judges learn how to organise their squads so as to take full advantage of their riot shields. By pulling together in a tight shield wall, every member gains mutual protection from his squad. The riot judge can organise a number of characters into a Defensive Shield equal to his character level as a standard action. All characters must be within 5 ft. of another and all must be armed with riot shields. Each gains a +2 bonus to their Defence Value while the Defensive Shield is maintained. They may only move 5 ft. per round while doing this.

Counter Charge: Small squads of judges make tempting targets for large mobs. At 8th level, the riot squad judge learns to Counter Charge an attacking enemy, lessening their advantage in melee combat. If charged by an enemy, the riot squad judge and any ally within 30 ft. of him may opt to Counter Charge. They count as charging the enemy and gain the usual +2 charge bonus to their attack rolls. In addition, the enemy does not receive their +2 charge bonus to attack rolls. Counter Charge may be combined with the Shield Rush class feature.

The Jaeger Squad Commando

Few Citi-Def units have a jaeger squad, but those who do include such men in their ranks are often considered to be elite forces. Each member of the jaeger squad is a full-time Citi-Def soldier who has dedicated himself to protecting his block against all enemies. Training hard in infiltration skills and the disruption of communications, the jaeger squad is as close to a commando unit as any Citi-Def is likely to get. Though still far from the highly disciplined judges, members of the jaeger squad gain a great deal of respect from other soldiers of their Citi-Def unit and can actually prove to be quite lethal in block wars.

Hit Die: d10.

Requirements

To qualify to become a jaeger squad commando, a citizen must fulfil all the following criteria.

Base Attack Bonus: +5.
Skills: Hide 6 ranks, Knowledge (military) 6 ranks, Medical 4 ranks, Move Silently 9 ranks, Technical 6 ranks.
Feats: Combat Reflexes, Endurance, Toughness,

The Jaeger Squad Commando

Level	Base Attack Bonus	Fort Save	Ref Save	Will Save	Special
1	+1	+2	+0	+0	Silent Killer, Sneak Attack +1d6
2	+2	+3	+0	+0	Defeat the Odds
3	+3	+3	+1	+1	Sneak Attack +2d6
4	+4	+4	+1	+1	Resist Mass Arrest
5	+5	+4	+1	+1	Sneak Attack +3d6

Weapon Focus.
Special: Must be a serving member of a Citi-Def unit.

Class Skills

The jaeger squad commando's class skills (and the key ability for each skill) are Balance (Dex), Climb (Str), Computer Use (Int), Hide (Dex), Jump (Str), Knowledge (military) (Int), Listen (Wis), Medical (Wis), Move Silently (Dex), Search (Int), Spot (Wis), Swim (Str), and Technical (Int).

Skill points at each level: 4 + Int modifier.

Class Features

All of the following are class features of the jaeger squad commando prestige class.

Silent Killer: The primary requirement for any jaeger squad commando is the ability to close quietly with a target before he launches an attack and most spend many hours training hard to succeed in this. The jaeger squad commando receives a competence bonus equal to his

The Block Champion

Level	Base Attack Bonus	Fort Save	Ref Save	Will Save	Special
1	+1	+2	+0	+0	Citizen's Champion
2	+2	+3	+0	+0	Gather Squad
3	+3	+3	+1	+1	Gather Mob
4	+4	+4	+1	+1	Resist Mass Arrest
5	+5	+4	+1	+1	Incite War

class level to all Hide and Move Silently checks he is called to make.

Sneak Attack: Members of the jaeger squad pride themselves on their prowess to assassinate enemy officers and unit leaders. If the jaeger squad commando can catch an enemy by surprise, flat-footed or by flanking, he can make a sneak attack. The extra damage a jaeger squad commando deals to an enemy he has managed to sneak attack is listed on the table below but he may only make sneak attacks in melee combat or against targets within 30 ft. with a ranged weapon. Sneak attacks may not be made against non-living targets or those immune to critical hits.

Defeat the Odds: Members of the jaeger squad are trained to operate in small squads and are well used to facing enemies who greatly outnumber them. At 2nd level, any attacker of a unit led by the jaeger squad commando will count as being of one size class less on the Outmatching Table. A unit three times the size of that being led by the jaeger squad commando, for example, will count as only being twice the size.

Resist Mass Arrest: The jaeger squad commando is utterly dedicated to his block and will not halt his mission, even if ordered to do so by a judge. Any judge attempting to arrest a unit led by the jaeger squad commando will have the result of his Mass Arrest check halved.

The Block Champion

Most citizens are, in their own way, fiercely loyal to their cityblock. A small fraction, however, take this loyalty to an utter extreme. They live, breathe and fight for their block above all else, and are often well known to the Justice Department as troublemakers. The block champion is often little more than a bully who likes to think he takes care of his own and lets the rest of the drokking world go to hell. He is at the forefront of any escalating tensions between blocks and is often responsible for outright block warfare. The citizens of the cityblock, however, tend to look up to their champion for both leadership in times of trouble and as a means to right any wrongs they believe they have suffered, cheering him on as he gets into continuous brawls with the champions of other blocks. In a city of 400 million people where true individuality is hard to achieve, the block champion has succeeded in developing his own sense of worth.

Hit Die: d8.

BEHIND THE JUDGES, BLOCK MOBS MET LIKE HUMAN BATTERING RAMS. FIGHTING WITH THE REMNANTS OF **DAN TANNA BLOCK** WERE THE **BETTY CROCKER** BLOCKERS –

RIKKI-RIKKI-RIKKI!

CROCKER 'EM!

AGAINST THEM, THE CONCERTED MIGHT OF **HENRY KISSINGER, RIKKI FULTON** AND **ENID BLYTON!**

ALL THE WAY WITH HENRY K– AAAGH!

Requirements

To qualify to become a block champion, a citizen must fulfil all the following criteria.

Base Attack Bonus: +6.
Skills: Intimidate 10 ranks, Streetwise 10 ranks.
Feats: Great Fortitude, Toughness.
Special: Must have lived within the same cityblock for at least 6 months. If he permanently moves away from this block, it will take a full 6 months to reacquire any class features gained as a block champion.

Class Skills

The block champion's class skills (and the key ability for each skill) are Bluff (Cha), Climb (Str), Craze (any) (various), Intimidate (Cha), Jump (Str), and Streetwise (Wis).

Skill points at each level: 4 + Int modifier.

Class Features

All of the following are class features of the block champion prestige class.

Citizen's Champion: The block champion is well known to his fellow citizens and has a measure of respect from them. Whenever leading a unit comprising citizens from his own block, the block champion grants a morale bonus equal to his class level to all attack and damage rolls they make.

Gather Squad: Upon reaching 2nd level, the block champion may, once per week, gather a group of citizens from his own block and launch a tirade against a rival block. Eager to support their block champion, many citizens will support him in taking action against this block that has obviously got away with too much for too long. If the block champion spends one minute making a speech to any group of citizens, he will incite 1d20 x his class level of them to violence against the targeted block.

Dredd's Comportment

'Pick off their leaders. The rest will lose stomach for the fight.'

On Mobs

This ability will only work on citizens who are residents of the same block as the block champion and will last for no more than one hour, after which the citizens drift back to their own apartments. They will eagerly follow the block champion in any action against the enemy block, so long as the block champion actually leads them, before drifting back to their apartments.

Gather Mob: As he reaches 3rd level, the block champion is likely to have become one of the most famous citizens in his block and most residents will have at east heard of him. He can use his influence to gather far larger mobs than before. Gather Mob works in the same way as Gather Squad, but 4d20 x his character level of citizens will be raised into a unit, and they will happily follow the block champion for a period of 1d3 hours.

Resist Mass Arrest: The block champion is utterly dedicated to his block and will not shy away from any action against a rival block, even if ordered to do so by a judge. Any judge attempting to arrest a unit led by the block champion will have the result of his Mass Arrest check halved.

Incite War: The Justice Department will likely have extensive files on the block champion by the time he has reached 5th level for he is truly a dangerous citizen. So popular is he in his home block that he can rally almost every citizen living there to fight against their rivals. Once per month, the block champion can automatically start a block war between his own block and one rival of his choice. This takes a full 24 hours to prepare, as he rallies support and makes plans. Note that the judges are well aware of his influence by this time and so spot arrests will likely become a way of life for the block champion.

New Feats

The introduction of block wars and riots can add a whole new dimension to games of Judge Dredd, whether your players are engaging in judge or perp-based campaigns. A new set of feats are detailed here, allowing characters to specialise in creating massive amounts of destruction or co-ordinate the actions of others far more effectively.

Additional Lieutenant (General)

The character is unusually charismatic and is able to convince a second trusted lieutenant to join his street gang, helping it grow and expand.

Prerequisites: Leadership, the character must be of at least 9th level and be a gang leader.
Benefits: When this feat is selected, the character immediately gains a second lieutenant to join his street gang. This new lieutenant starts off at one level lower than indicated on page 151 of the *Judge Dredd Rulebook*.

Advanced Leadership (General)

The character has actually studied hard to learn what makes a good leader and, in conjunction with his sheer force of personality, can command large forces in battle.
Prerequisites: Leadership, the character must be of at least 12th level.
Benefits: Having this feat allows a character to command an entire force, comprising several different units simultaneously, as described in Chapter 3. In addition, if he is the leader of a street gang, he will gain double the normal number of gang members indicated on page 151 of the *Judge Dredd Rulebook*.

Armour Penetration (Judge)

A single weapon is chosen, such as street cannon or Lawgiver. The character is especially good at bypassing armour with this weapon, seeking weak points in heavy plating whenever he attacks.
Prerequisite: Weapon Focus (same weapon as that of Armour Penetration), base attack bonus of +6 or higher.
Benefit: The character increases the Armour Piercing score of his weapon by +1. This feat may only be used with ranged weapons if the target is within 60 feet.
Special: The character can gain this feat multiple times. Each time the feat is taken, a new weapon is selected.

Armour Specialisation (General)

The character is adept in combat, having lived to tell of some of the roughest block wars and riots to have sprung up in Mega-City One. He has learnt how to roll with blows and can instinctively turn to catch each strike with the thickest and most well protected part of his armour.
Prerequisites: Base attack bonus of +4 or higher.
Benefit: So long as the character is wearing armour of some description, he may increase his Damage Reduction score by +1 against all melee attacks. This feat may not be used while the character is flat-footed or surprised, nor is it of any use against ranged attacks.

Command (General)

Used to being in a position of some small authority, the character is capable of commanding others to act spontaneously to the sound of his voice.

Dredd's Comportment

'No matter what the cause, it's gotta be stamped on – hard!'

On Riots

Prerequisites: Iron Will, Charisma 15+.
Benefit: The character may approach any group of citizens, who may not have levels in any other class, numbering no more than his character level +10. These citizens must be witnessing a rumble, riot or block war. After spending 1 minute engaging in a passionate speech concerning the evils of one side or another active in the violence, the character must make a Charisma check at DC 15. If successful, he may instruct the citizens to perform any single task. Such tasks may not be immediately suicidal (such as leaping off a block or charging a Manta Prowl Tank armed only with clubs) and must be possible to complete within one hour. The character could, for example, command the citizens to join in one side of a block war, conduct a flank attack against an enemy's assault team or infiltrate the foundations of an enemy block. The character need not stay with the citizens to conduct the task and they will perform it to the best of their ability. If the character does stay with these citizens, he can continue using this feat to give them further commands.

Duck & Weave (General)

Having been involved in several riots or block wars in the past, the character has learnt to keep his head down when shots start flying overhead. Unconsciously taking advantage of every scrap of cover from burnt-out vehicles, overturned kneepad stalls and even other citizens, the character can carry out other tasks while under a greater degree of safety.
Prerequisites: Base attack bonus +2 or higher, Dex 13+.
Benefit: So long as the character is not caught flat-footed or surprised, he will always count as being in one level of cover better than he actually is. A character standing behind a bike (one-quarter cover), for example, will actually count as being in one-half cover. One in an enclosed vehicle (nine-tenths cover) will be impossible to

target. This feat may not be used if the character is not in any cover at all.

Improved Mass Arrest (Judge)

There are few citizens willing to challenge an experienced judge unless they are part of a mob. However, even the largest mob may quail before the authority of this judge.

Prerequisites: Improved Mass Arrest, Cha 15+.
Benefit: The character may double the result of any Mass Arrest checks he makes.

Improved Weapon Focus (General)

The character is exceptionally good at wielding one type of weapon and is able to thrust home lightning-fast attacks that defy rational explanation. He is truly a master of combat.

Prerequisites: Proficient with weapon, Weapon Focus, base attack bonus +12 or higher.
Benefit: Improved Weapon Focus may only be taken for a weapon type already chosen for the Weapon Focus feat. From this point, the character will gain a +2 bonus to all attack rolls made with the selected weapon. This bonus replaces that gained with Weapon Focus and they do not stack.
Special: A character can gain this feat multiple times. Its effects do not stack. Each time the feat is selected, it applies to a new weapon.

Inspire Loyalty (General)

Having fought alongside his allies through thick and thin, many now look to the character with great respect. They will always follow his commands, regardless of the consequences.
Prerequisites: Advanced Leadership, Command.
Benefit: Any unit led by the character in mass combat will automatically pass any Morale checks it is called upon to make.

Martyr (General)

Rumbles, riots and block wars bring out both the best and worst in citizens and judges. Insanely heroic acts may be performed that defy belief though their success is rarely enjoyed by the characters attempting them.
Benefit: The character will automatically succeed in any one action that takes one round or less to perform. This may be scoring maximum damage against a Pat-Wagon, setting fuses on a complicated set of explosives or anything else the Games Master deems suitable.

However, the character will also immediately and automatically be killed while performing this action. The Games Master will determine a suitably heroic end for the character which, using the examples above, may be the Pat-Wagon exploding, catching the character in the blast, or the explosives detonating as he sets them.

Mass Arrest (Judge)

The judge is a dominating presence on the street, able to arrest dozens of rioting citizens at once with nothing more than a few harsh words.

Prerequisites: Improved Arrest, Menacing Presence, Nerves of Steel.
Benefit: The character is able to use the Mass Arrest rules described on p23.

Shot on the Wing (General)

The character is adept at using small personal flying devices, such as jetpacks, batgliders and para-gliders. He can control them almost instinctively, allowing him to concentrate on other actions.
Benefit: The character can make any Craze (batgliding), (jetpacking), (para-gliding) or similar check as a free action, allowing him to perform other, more complicated actions simultaneously.

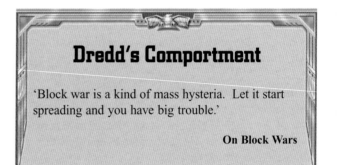

Dredd's Comportment

'Block war is a kind of mass hysteria. Let it start spreading and you have big trouble.'

On Block Wars

Weapons & Equipment

Few citizens plan a block war in advance and most take to the streets with whatever weaponry and equipment they are able to grab or steal. A tiny minority, however, can sometimes plan their role in a forthcoming block war extremely carefully. Those who pay attention to the mutterings and general mood of citizens around them can sometimes be perceptive enough to recognise when a block war becomes inevitable, while others may actually instigate their own civil disturbance.

Engaging in a riot or block war requires very different tactics and equipment to a common brawl or firefight. Huge mobs need to be engaged decisively and heavily-armoured judges need to be defeated quickly, before they can begin arresting large numbers of allies. The wise perp, knowing that a block war is inevitable, stocks up on specialised equipment, guaranteeing he will remain alive and at liberty to continue his criminal schemes.

Weaponry

Hand Gun, Cursed Earth Eagle: Manufactured in Texas City, the Cursed Earth Eagle is considered by many perps to be the most powerful hand gun ever designed,

Hand Gun, Cursed Earth Eagle

though some alleged experts are quick to cite various Sov-made weapons for this honour. The extremely large calibre used by this hand gun allows it to literally blast an enemy apart, whatever armour he is wearing, but also serves to make the weapon extremely intimidating to any citizen finding himself at the wrong end of the barrel. The large shells employed, however, severely limit the amount of ammunition that can be carried in a single magazine, and so the Cursed Earth Eagle is rarely used in extended firefights. The magazine of the Cursed Earth Eagle holds 6 rounds.

High Velocity Rifle, Walther Mitsubishi MarksMan Mk II: Though designed for accuracy at range, the incredible velocities at which the MarksMan Mk II propels its relatively small shells is sufficient to penetrate even the armour of a riot squad judge. This has made the rifle an extremely attractive weapon for self-styled judge killers, as well as perps who expect to regularly engage in combat against Justice Department personnel. Against less well-armoured targets, however, there are far more efficient weapons readily available on the black market. The magazine of the MarksMan Mk II holds 12 rounds.

Mega-Explosives: Based on the principle of the hi-ex pack, this group of weapons represent explosives of several orders of magnitude greater in potency. Difficult and expensive to get hold of, the larger mega-explosives are capable of blasting through bank vaults, penetrating thick armour and even bringing down an entire cityblock,

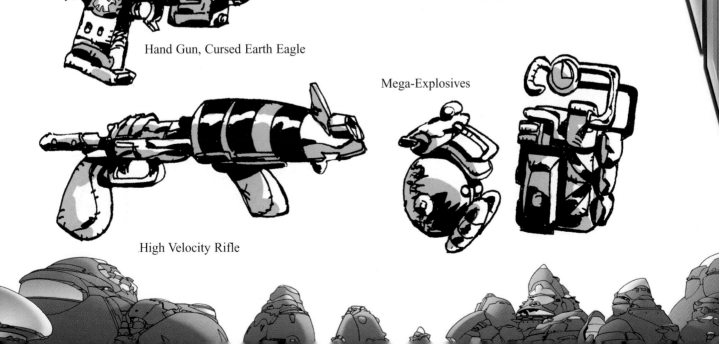

Mega-Explosives

High Velocity Rifle

Equipment

New Weaponry

Weapon	Cost	Black Market Cost	Damage	Armour Piercing
Pistol Weapons				
Small				
Hand Gun, Cursed Earth Eagle	3,625 cr.	12,750 cr.	4d6	12
Rifle Weapons				
Large				
High-Velocity Rifle, Walther Mitsubishi MarksMan Mk II	6,500 cr.	22,750 cr.	3d6	14
Heavy Weapons				
Large				
Missile Defence Laser, Mauley Hard Light DX	29,500 cr.	93,000 cr.	4d10	20
Scatter Cannon, General Arms M276	9,750 cr.	29,000 cr.	3d6	4
Exotic Weapons				
Mega-Explosives, small	675 cr.	3,250 cr.	4d10	17
Mega-Explosives, medium	1,250 cr.	6,000 cr.	6d10	18
Mega-Explosives, large	2,250 cr.	10,000 cr.	8d10	19
Mega-Explosives, huge	3,000 cr.	16,500 cr.	10d10	20

if carefully placed and grouped together. Each explosive device may either be set by timer (up to one year's delay) or by remote, with a maximum range of 3,000 ft. They must be set carefully, taking one minute, and may not be thrown. All mega-explosives require the Weapon Proficiency (exotic – mega-explosives) feat to use successfully. Characters attempting to use mega-

explosives without this feat have a 10% chance of detonating the explosives as they are being set.

Missile Defence Laser, Mauley Hard Light DX: The technology to be found in the missile defence lasers present in most Citi-Def armouries throughout Mega-City One is incredibly sophisticated. It is a triumph of the

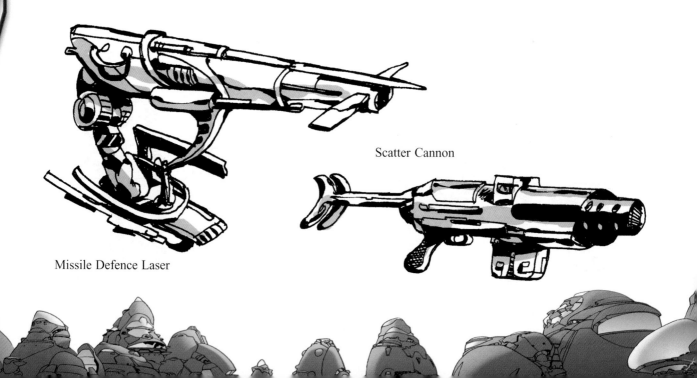

Scatter Cannon

Missile Defence Laser

Scenario Hooks & Ideas

The mass combat system presented in *The Rookie's Guide to Block Wars* provides the Games Master with great potential to come up with some truly memorable scenarios for his players. Characters of all levels, judge and citizen alike, may be challenged by huge mobs no matter how experienced or well equipped they are. In addition, players may get a real boost from defeating the latest criminal mastermind or rival to come their way, but there is nothing quite like being involved in a full-scale riot or block war!

Presented here is a short jump-off list of scenario hooks and ideas that a Games Master may use to introduce the mass combat system into an existing campaign.

Just Struttin About

You need not have a full-scale block war to introduce the mass combat system to your players and, until everyone is comfortable with the new rules, it is best to limit the scale of battles that take place. Keep the number of combatants low and just have one unit on each side to begin with. An ideal introduction that can be used for even low level characters is a simple rumble between two juve street gangs. The individual combatants will be relatively weak, giving the players some leeway while they get used to the rules and there will be few modifiers and other factors to take into account as they fight. Such a rumble may take place between the player's own street gang (either one they lead, or one they have become allied to) and a rival, or a patrol of judges may be called to calm a disturbance as two gangs begin to dispute their territories. When dealing with juve gangs, you need little real reason to start a rumble, as they are all bored and just spoiling for a fight with anyone foolish enough to stand in their way.

Practising Citi-Def

Though most blocks have a Citi-Def unit, few are truly taken seriously. Most are filled with bored citizens desperate to emulate the glory of their favourite action-vid star, though the reality is usually more boredom as they are endlessly drilled and schooled. Once in a while, however, a Citi-Def officer may appear to lead an ailing unit. Realising that only real action will truly make his men combat-ready, the officer will start to create highly detailed plans to attack another block, a vital Meg-Way junction or even a Justice Department armoury! Many will lead their men with the intention of only simulating combat but with a great deal of high-powered weaponry in the hands of bored citizens, only disaster can result from such exercises.

Power Dispute

It is truly amazing how little it takes to spark off a block war, though judges quickly learn never to be taken unawares. Though Mega-City One has some of the greatest power resources available on Earth, there is still a finite amount to be spread among 400 million citizens. Inevitably, power shortages occur, whether through criminal activity, lack of maintenance or simple high demand. It has been known for neighbouring blocks on the same power grid to actually effect one another in terms of the current they draw at specific times. One block, for example, may have a slightly higher priority on

the power grid than an adjacent building and so, when the majority of its citizens tune in their Tri-D to see Sob Story every week, the extra current drawn can actually cause a black-out in their neighbours' block. When this begins to happen with any great degree of regularity, tensions between blocks can run extremely high and block war may only be hours away.

Jetball Matches

The citizens of Mega-City One are keen to latch onto any diversion or interest that can make them feel that they 'belong' to something. Blocks are a readily identifiable method of building these divisions in the population but others do exist – Jetball is an extremely popular sport with the league matches between the biggest teams guaranteeing huge audiences across the entire city. Judges always patrol in force at such events, for they know all too well how one minor incident on the pitch or one bad call by a referee droid can spark riots across whole sectors as citizens release the fury of their team's defeat in the most basic ways possible.

Juves Versus Eldsters

It is a sad fact of life in Mega-City One that juves simply no longer respect their elders. With the rapid progression of medical science, a citizen can expect to live for an extremely long time, and still maintain the majority of their faculties and physical abilities while doing so. The eldsters of the city are therefore quite mobile and far from defenceless. A simple incident, such as a juve throwing something at an eldster's servodroid can cause even centenarian citizens to band together for mutual protection. When they next encounter a juve, the eldsters will be likely to swing with their walking sticks first and ask questions later, leading to inevitable retaliation from other juves. Things can degenerate very rapidly as more juves and eldsters enter the fray from neighbouring blocks.

Charles Darwin Goes Ape II

There is no need to restrict the mass combat system presented in this book to human characters alone and a great deal of fun can be had by constructing units formed by creatures found within the Creeps chapter of the *Judge Dredd Rulebook*. The apes of the Jungle, for instance, could easily rally behind an influential and charismatic gorilla with plans to put humans in their rightful place – under the heel of true apes! Leading an army of apes out

of the Jungle, a surprise attack may well allow the apes to take over an entire block, which would then serve not only as a base of operations but as a beacon to attract yet more apes to the growing army. Perps will likely find their best laid plans ruined by such an invasion, while judge characters could have a serious fight on their hands as they try to restore Law and order to a block that has literally gone ape!

Mutieland

An expedition into the Cursed Earth can rapidly turn into a disaster for a patrol of judges or group of citizens looking to further their criminal activities. Gangs and whole armies of mutants await to prey on the unwary and the largest dinosaurs can pose a serious problem for even a large group of well-armed characters. You could have the players visit several townships and settlements in the heart of the Cursed Earth while being pursued by the agents of a large mutant force. Alternatively, they could get caught up in an ongoing feud between two forces in the Cursed Earth. Once the players delay or become trapped in a single settlement, an entire army can move in for the kill. The players will have to organise the defences of an entire town with weaponry that is likely far more primitive than that found within Mega-City One. A series of desperate combats can be fought out as the attackers constantly probe for weaknesses or, if you have a large enough table and map, you could play out the entire siege as one gigantic mass combat involving thousands of mutants and dozens of units.

Come the Kleggs

Just one or two kleggs can cause even an experienced patrol of judges a great deal of trouble, as their natural strength, resilience and access to the dreaded klegg assault cannon will create a whole world of pain for characters who just rush in to any combat. A whole mercenary force of them organised into a single unit may well be undefeatable without calling in major ordnance like Manta Prowl Tanks and H-Wagons! A klegg spaceship may be forced to crash-land into the heart of Mega-City One after being damaged by an orbital platform or some criminal organisation may actually be mad enough to try to hire a mercenary band of these aliens in an attempt to wipe out the opposition. Kleggs are never subtle and, knowing the hatred borne of them by both judges and citizens after their actions in the reign of Chief Judge Caligula, will be unlikely to surrender or compromise even when faced with superior opposition.

Multiple Targets

A patrol of judges could be kept on their toes when they are placed in command of an operation to pin down the latest activities of the sector's largest criminal organisation. Dozens of mo-pads, roadliners and juggers have been hijacked and are now being used to ferry large numbers of goons all over the sector to quickly strike at judges and innocent citizens alike. The players will have to combat a large number of fast-moving vehicles which can deploy fairly large units to cause havoc before melting away. The organisation's real goal, however, is actually the local Justice Department armoury – just when the judges have their attention focussed on the mobile groups of goons, the real force will appear, comprising well-equipped professionals all eager to get their hands on the latest Justice Department equipment. With judges strewn all over the sector in a vain effort to combat the diversionary goons, the armoury could well be left wide open to concerted attack. Beware – this scenario could require a very large map with a very large scale!

Renegade Droids

Construction meks are supposed to have 100%-reliable fail safes to ensure they do not go rogue, but citizens with criminal intentions may delight in re-programming several of these destructive machines. Use the normal mass combat rules and include perhaps a dozen such robots within the same unit. Such a force would be capable of breaking through to the most heavily defended bank vault and will be able to give even a patrol of senior judges a few problems. For added amusement, have the perp retrofit the construction meks with heavy lasers to act as air defence against the inevitable H-Wagons the players will wish to call as back-up.

Running with the Perps

The high arrest rate of the judges in Mega-City One ensures there is a significant traffic of successful perps attempting to escape judicial punishment to other city states or even other worlds. The judges work hard to bring down all perp-running vehicles and H-Wagon crews enjoy a great deal of success in such operations. A crashed perp-runner shuttle or hover vehicle will be packed full of desperate and likely well-armed perps eager to retain their freedom. Any operational weapons on the vehicle will be turned upon responding street judge patrols and the escaping perps will be happy to work together as a cohesive unit for a brief period of time until they can melt away for another attempt to leave the city.

Cursed Earth Immigrants

Despite the highly efficient defence screen protecting Mega-City One from invaders originating in the Cursed Earth, there are lapses – wall guns may be sabotaged, attacks can be made on ruined wall sections or defences may simply be overwhelmed by sheer numbers. Regardless of how it happens, those breaking into the city will be desperate, predatory and likely highly confused by their surroundings – in short, a danger to the well-being of any decent citizen! Such a scenario can be scaled up or down to suit the level and capabilities of the players, from a large pack of stray dog vultures, to a veritable invasion force of mutated wall hoppers!

STUMM GAS – ITS CHOKING VAPOURS BROUGHT NAUSEA AND UNCONSCIOUSNESS. IN ONE CASE IN EVERY 250, IT ALSO CAUSED **DEATH**...

BETTER FIFTY STIFFS THAN FIFTY THOUSAND, FOGERTY!

Madonna Ciccone & Cher Sky Rise

The last couple of chapters of *The Rookie's Guide to Block Wars* focus on two cityblocks and their residents, completely detailed and ready for use in your own campaign. The Madonna Ciccone cityblock and Cher Sky Rise have been rivals since the former was built and, while a full scale block war has yet to erupt, tensions are beginning to reach breaking point. Perfect territory to introduce your players to the mass combat system detailed in this supplement!

You can use the information here as a focal point for a complete scenario, or have the two blocks recurring time and again throughout a campaign so players begin to know both buildings and the citizens living within as well as they do their own town. Judges may find themselves constantly called to resolve disputes and arrest perps for a series of trivial offences that gradually become more frequent and more serious as both Madonna Ciccone block and Cher Sky Rise gear themselves up for a full-blown block war. Citizen characters may have criminal or business interests within either (or both!) blocks, or may be residents themselves. Either way, a coming block war will likely disrupt any long term plans they have and force them to reconsider or even move on. Clever players, however, may find a way to take advantage of the continuing civil disturbance.

Sector 190, MegWest

Madonna Ciccone block and Cher Sky Rise are both located in Sector 190, close to the city wall that shields citizens from the dangers of the Cursed Earth. Many supplements and scenarios for the Judge Dredd roleplaying game are based in Sector 190, which will grow and develop to become a living, breathing place in which to base entire campaigns. Games Masters may safely start their players within this sector, assured that they will receive a continuing level of support in the setting.

A Games Master may, however, choose to base his campaign in a completely different sector of Mega-City One. In such a case, he may use material based in Sector 190 as a basis for his own characters and scenarios. The Games Master may, for example, take both blocks presented in this chapter, change their names and introduce completely different characters living within them – once you start running a game of Judge Dredd, Mega-City One becomes *your* city to do with as you wish. Have fun!

Cher Sky Rise

The Cher Sky Rise was a triumph of design during its day, towering above other blocks in Mega-City One. The latest construction technologies allowed it to soar nearly 200 levels into the sky and house thousands of citizens. Now, it is over fifty years old and starting to show its age. Despite numerous refits and structural redesigning, the pre-atomic Cher is bordering on being reclassified as a slum block and despite having fiercely loyal residents, few are under the illusion of their block seriously competing with its neighbours in terms of comfort, security and facilities.

Originally part of the Twin Sky Rise complex, Cher once stood next to Sonny Cityblock and together they housed nearly one hundred thousand citizens, a monument to their architect's vision and skill. For decades, the Housing Department struggled to keep both from turning into slum blocks through a succession of updates and renovation projects. Cher was to prove durable enough to survive the passage of time, but Sonny gradually began to lag far beyond as more and more credits were fed into its counterpart at its own expense. In 2120, the Housing Department ordered the demolition of Sonny and began the construction of the new, high-technology Madonna Ciccone cityblock in its place.

Disputes are both predictable and common between the citizens of Cher and Madonna Ciccone. The citizens of Cher are somewhat jealous of their new neighbours, living in relative luxury while they have to contend with constantly malfunctioning lifts, a second rate shopping mall and medical facilities that are barely adequate. For their part, the residents of Madonna Ciccone hardly appreciate living next to a towering eyesore that is a slum block in all but name. Conflicts, however, are typically confined to name calling across the Tweenblock Plaza and the inevitable skirmishes between juve street gangs. Local judges keep a close watch on the situation that has certainly not been helped by more and more Cher citizens beginning to visit the Madonna Ciccone shopping malls which boast higher prices but also the latest fashions and gadgets.

Madonna Ciccone Block
Sector 190, MegWest
Built: 2122
Type: Cityblock
Levels: 223
Population: 66,900
Citi-Def: 1,100, 1st level
Damage Reduction: 18
Structural Hit Points: 44,600

Cher Sky Rise
Sector 190, MegWest
Built: 2068
Type: Pre-atomic block
Levels: 192
Population: 48,000
Citi-Def: 900, 2nd level
Damage Reduction: 16
Structural Hit Points: 29,100

Throughout the fifty years of the Cher Sky Rise's history, its citizens have picked a fight with just about every block in the area and many are veterans of full-scale block wars, having served time in the cubes and now returned to their home. Increased judge patrols and regular solitary confinements have tempered violence in recent years but, instead of resolving the situation, frustrations have merely been bottled up with tensions rising day by day. Sector House 190 marks Madonna Ciccone and Cher Sky Rise as a high-potential trouble spot – for the judges, it is not a question of if a block war will erupt, but when.

The exterior of the Cher Sky Rise clearly demonstrates the block's slip into a slum. Its half of the Tweenblock Plaza is rarely cleaned or cared for and is strewn with all manner of debris and rubbish. The walls of the block itself are covered with the work of juve scrawlers and typically feature insults to Madonna Ciccone blockers in the largest and brightest way conceivable. Because of Cher's low priority in the sector, clean-up crews rarely visit more often than once a month and so the graffiti remains a constant source of rising tension within Madonna Ciccone.

Inside, life is of poor quality, with many levels designated as no-go areas by the few remaining block security guards. Weaker citizens spend most of their lives within their apartments, fearing to step out side of their doors and into the halls controlled by juve gangs, such as the notorious Spectres and their smaller rivals. Educational and medical facilities have been allowed to slip into an advanced state of dilapidation and the constant renovation programmes once enjoyed by the block that allowed it to keep pace with its neighbours have long since been abandoned. The last was an exterior cluster of anti-grav chutes that would have allowed free and easy passage to any part of the block. The project was never finished, however, and now citizens must rely on decrepit lifts or, failing that, the hundreds of flights of stairs.

Despite their poor style of living and propensity to prey upon one another, the residents of the Cher Sky Rise are fiercely independent and all too ready to view outsiders as 'The Enemy'. It has been a long time since they were able to release their frustrations in any meaningful way and so it may only take one tiny incident to spark a full assault on the current object of tension – Madonna Ciccone.

Madonna Ciccone Block

The citizens of Madonna Ciccone enjoy a wealth of facilities and though it is no luxy-block, most would agree it is the next best thing – especially as apartments are provided free by the Housing Department. Barely two years old, Madonna Ciccone is a shining example of the life Mega-City One can provide for its citizens, providing credits and other resources are available. The main shopping mall alone covers the bottom six levels of the block and many other smaller malls are strewn throughout the higher levels. Medical and educational facilities are among the best available in Sector 190, ensuring the residents are well cared for, content and long-lived. The only real detriment to living in Madonna Ciccone is the presence of the nauseating Cher Sky Rise just across the Tweenblock Plaza.

It takes a good while for citizens of a new block to develop the traditional loyalty to their home readily found elsewhere and those dwelling in Madonna Ciccone have had precious few rallying points with which to develop this unity. Local judges are aware that the Cher Sky Rise is beginning to provide just such a focus. The Madonna Ciccone half of the Tweenblock Plaza shared by both cityblocks is kept in near immaculate condition, with a fine garden park to while away lazy afternoons, a well-protected vehicle lot and even a private security station funded by all residents. This is in stark contrast to the Cher Sky Rise's half which resembles something close to an urban wasteland.

At present, however, Madonna Ciccone still shows all the signs of a developing residential environment – many apartments on the higher levels are still empty and awaiting new arrivals, membership of the Citi-Def is not popular and there are few real juve gangs. Though clashes between the blocks have been more or less restricted to juves and their pranks, the gradual increase of Cher citizens entering 'their' block to enjoy the treats of the huge shopping mall have provoked some strong reactions. It is apparent that the hired security guards are being pressured to deny all access to Madonna Ciccone, though this is technically illegal. In spite of that, the guards know full well where their monthly credits come from, and a group of Cher blockers being barred from entering Madonna Ciccone's half of the Tweenblock Plaza may be all that is required to spark violence.

Despite being a little taller, having access to updated weaponry in its Citi-Def armoury, and housing more than half as many citizens again as the Cher Sky Rise, there are some cooler heads within Madonna Ciccone who have little wish to provoke their neighbours. Cher blockers are, overall, far more united than the more numerous Madonna Ciccone citizens and possess larger (and more desperate) street gangs. Their Citi-Def has several veterans of block wars in the past and it is all too apparent that some are just spoiling for another fight. It is with some regularity, then, that petitions sweep through the citizens of Madonna Ciccone, pleading with the Housing Department to simply demolish the ugly sky rise. There is little hope of success, however, until resources can be made available to construct a replacement block. So far, no Cher blocker has discovered the petitions made to the Housing Department but it is no secret within Madonna Ciccone – once again, this is another potential flash-point should they find out that the Ciccone blockers have the temerity to actually attempt to eradicate their home without having the decency to try it in a full blown war.

Citi-Def Units

Should it ever come to block war between the Cher Sky Rise and Madonna Ciccone, the opposing Citi-Def units may prove to be remarkably well balanced against each other. Though the Ciccone Citi-Def is small compared to other blocks of similar size, due to the residents being newcomers to the area, it still outnumbers that of the Cher unit. In addition, it has access to far superior weaponry. The Cher Citi-Def, however, has far more experienced soldiers in its ranks, as well as a group of tough jaeger squad commandos who will likely prove decisive in any action. Add to that the number of street gangs based within the Sky Rise and it quickly becomes apparent that the citizens of Madonna Ciccone will have quite a fight on their hands should Cher blockers ever decide to launch an assault.

Detailed here are the Citi-Def units available to both Madonna Ciccone and Cher Sky Rise. Games Masters are welcome to use these units 'as it' in scenarios involving the two blocks, or may simply view them as an example of how typical Citi-Def units may appear in Mega-City One.

Madonna Ciccone Citi-Def

Class: Citizen (Citi-Def soldier)
Level: 1   **Unit Size:** 1,100
Unit Hit Points: 1210 (+10% Toughness)
Unit Leader: None

Initiative: +1 (+1 Dex)
Attacks: Las-knife +0 melee or spit gun +1 ranged
Damage: Las-knife 1d6/10 or spit gun 2d6/6
DV: 11 (+1 Reflex)
Damage Reduction: 8 (shell jacket)
Special Abilities: None
Ability Scores: Str 10, Dex 12, Con 11, Int 10, Wis 9, Cha 10
Saves: Fort +0, Ref +1, Will -1
Feats: Endurance, Toughness

Malvern Turker

Officially, Malvern is the officer in command of the Madonna Ciccone Citi-Def, though he is more concerned with the inventory of the armoury and neatness of uniforms than any actual drills or fighting. He has managed to instil something resembling discipline in his unit and he works hard to actively recruit new members to the still small force but his abilities in combat are highly dubious and this inevitably affects the soldiers beneath him, especially as he has begun to divide his time between the unit and his new passion, batgliding. Overall, his Citi-Def are fairly well-equipped and smartly turned out but remain utterly inexperienced in any form of combat.

Citizen 6 (Citi-Def soldier); HD 6d6 (23); Init +1 (+1 Dex); Spd 30 ft.; DV 15 (+5 Reflex); Attack +5 las-knife (1d6/10), or +7 laser pistol (4d6/14); Fort +2, Ref +3, Will +2; Str 10, Dex 13, Con 11, Int 10, Wis 11, Cha 10.
Skills and feats: Appraise +6, Bluff +5, Climb +4, Computer Use +11, Concentration +4, Craze (batgliding) +7, Drive +6, Hide +5, Intimidate +3, Jump +3, Knowledge (military) +2, Listen +6, Medical +5, Pilot +5, Streetwise +4, Spot +9, Technical +6; Alertness, Emergency Stop, Luck of Grud, Skill Focus (computer use).
Possessions: Las-knife, laser pistol, shell jacket (DR 8).

Cher Sky Rise Citi-Def

Class: Citizen (Citi-Def soldier)
Level: 2   **Unit Size:** 780
Unit Hit Points: 1872 (+10% Constitution 13, +10% Toughness)
Unit Leader: None
Initiative: +1 (+1 Dex)
Attacks: Club +2 melee or stump gun +3 ranged
Damage: Club 1d8+1/0 or stump gun 2d6/2
DV: 11 (+1 Reflex)
Damage Reduction: 8 (shell jacket)
Special Abilities: None

Ability Scores: Str 13, Dex 12, Con 13, Int 9, Wis 8, Cha 11
Saves: Fort +1, Ref +1, Will -1
Feats: Toughness, Weapon Focus (stump gun)

'Colonel' Patty Smarman

Though the title of colonel is purely self-awarded, Patty is regarded by many in the Cher Sky Rise as the best commanding officer they have ever had in their Citi-Def. A veteran of several block wars in the past, Patty has dedicated her life to her unit and so would fight to the last if her block was to come under threat, whether this came from another block, the Housing Department demolition squads or the judges themselves. She regularly trains the soldiers in her command, and trains them hard. Few other blocks will willingly and openly challenge the Cher Sky Rise unless they believe they have a distinct advantage in either numbers or firepower – and preferably both.

Citi-Def officer 3/citizen 6 (Citi-Def soldier); HD 3d8+6d6+18 (53); Init +3 (+3 Dex); Spd 30 ft.; DV 15 (+5 Reflex); Attack +8 knife (1d6+1/2), or +12 heavy spit gun (3d6/8); Fort +7, Ref +8, Will +3; Str 12, Dex 17, Con 14, Int 10, Wis 10, Cha 14.
Skills and feats: Climb +9, Drive +13, Intimidate +14, Jump +11, Knowledge (military) +12, Medical +10, Search +2, Streetwise +10, Spot +11, Technical +10; Duck & Weave, Leadership, Lightning Reflexes, Skill Focus (intimidate), Weapon Focus (heavy spit gun).
Possessions: Heavy spit gun, knife, shell jacket (DR 8).

Cher Sky Rise Jaeger Squad

Class: Citizen (Citi-Def soldier)/jaeger squad commando **Level:** 7/1
Unit Size: 20
Unit Hit Points: 192 (+10% Constitution 12, +10% Toughness)
Unit Leader: None
Initiative: +2 (+2 Dex)
Attacks: Knife +8 melee or spit gun +9 ranged

Damage: Knife 1d6+2/2 or spit gun 2d6/2
DV: 14 (+4 Reflex)
Damage Reduction: 8 (shell jacket)
Special Abilities: Silent killer, sneak attack +1d6
Ability Scores: Str 15, Dex 14, Con 12, Int 10, Wis 10, Cha 11
Saves: Fort +5, Ref +4, Will +2
Feats: Combat Reflexes, Endurance, Toughness, Weapon Focus (spit gun)

Trigger Spetsnatz

Subordinate to Colonel Patty Smarman, Trigger is generally regarded as the most frightening man to live in the Cher Sky Rise. Leading the small but elite jaeger squad of the Citi-Def unit, Trigger seems to look for trouble with other blocks and has sparked off more than one block war in the past, landing him in the cubes for an extended stretch. Though at liberty now, the Justice Department is well aware of both his skills and attitude, and he is regularly 'harassed' as he calls it. It is rumoured that he once killed a judge with his bare hands but Colonel Patty works hard to keep him out of sight as much as possible, knowing she cannot risk losing him to the cubes once more if another block war erupts. Trigger is currently spending much of his time exploring the

Trigger
Spetznatz

Patty
Smarman

underground tunnel complex running below the Tweenblock Plaza, in search of a quick and easy route to the foundations of Madonna Ciccone. . .

Jaeger squad commando 5/citizen 7 (Citi-Def soldier); HD 5d10+7d6+27 (82); Init +2 (+2 Dex); Spd 30 ft.; DV 17 (+7 Reflex); Attack +15 las-knife (1d6+5/10), or +12 hand gun (3d6/4); Fort +8, Ref +7, Will +4 Str 20, Dex 15, Con 15, Int 9, Wis 12, Cha 14.
Skills and feats: Climb +14, Drive +4, Hide +17, Intimidate +15, Jump +19, Knowledge (military) +5, Medical +5, Move Silently +15, Streetwise +8, Spot +8, Technical +5; Combat Reflexes, Endurance, Leadership, Lightning Reflexes, Toughness, Weapon Focus (las-knife).
Possessions: Hand gun, las-knife, shell jacket (DR 8).

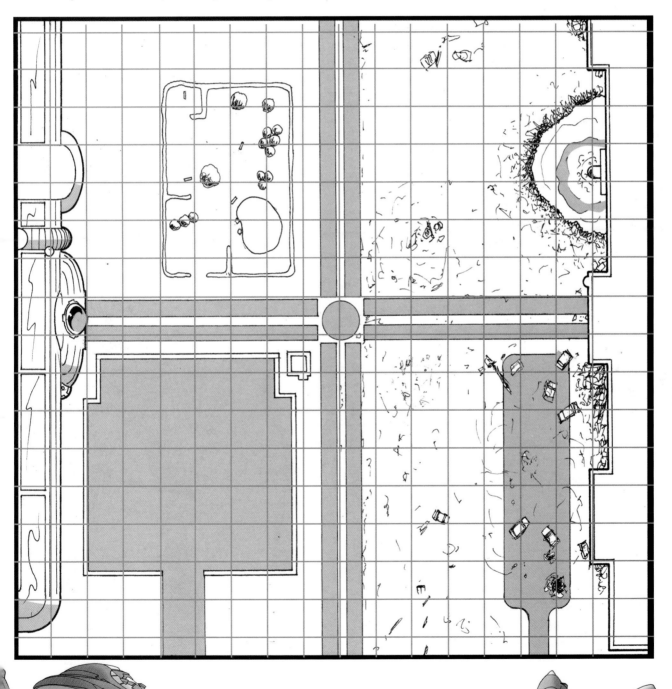

Street Gangs

This last chapter details six streets gangs, ready to painlessly slide into your own scenarios and campaigns with little work. Though all six are based in either the Cher Sky Rise or Madonna Ciccone blocks, they may be used in any block, street or sector with few changes. Each is related to the others in some way (usually as rivals!), thus providing a Games Master with an immediate set of protagonists with which to draw the players into a new scenario, be they judge or citizen characters. Each street gang is designed to interact with even low level characters (be wary of direct confrontations though), and yet be strong enough to take the role of a recurring nemesis or ally through several scenarios if the Games Master so desires.

As with the two cityblocks presented in the previous chapter, a Games Master can use these street gangs as part of a complete scenario, or have them appearing throughout a campaign so players start to learn about the types of personalities that inhabit Mega-City One. Judges may chance upon any of these street gangs during a rumble or may begin to learn about their activities during an ongoing investigation. Citizen characters may attempt to create alliances with some of these gangs in order to better facilitate their criminal interests, or may find themselves directly opposing some of the gang leaders as they try to muscle in on each other's territory. However these street gangs are met, the Games Master will find there is ample opportunity to introduce his players to the rigours of the mass combat system. Remember, everything in Mega-City One happens on a huge scale – what might be a small and simple firefight in any other roleplaying game can easily turn into a multiple block war in Judge Dredd!

The Spectres

The few new families who are assigned to live in the Cher Sky Rise will not be there long before they hear about the Spectres.

Headquartered in their leader's apartment on level 12 of the sky rise, they form the largest street gang for several blocks around by far and have become a mighty power block other perps can only aspire to. Unfortunately, they have also grown to the size where they are almost beyond the leadership of their gang leader, Ozmund Blue. Compared to other gangs, they have a massive income of credits every month, derived from a variety of protection rackets and petty crime, but much of it ends up in the hands of pilfering gang members rather than their leader. Despite this, the Spectres are a constant terror in the hallways of the sky rise and the Tweenblock Plaza and few other gangs will willing confront or challenge a member. The gang has been around, in one form or another, for several years now and has undergone several changes in leadership, but its great size ensures there are always enough members to keep going no matter how many splinter groups separate and break away to pursue their own interests. However, every other gang in

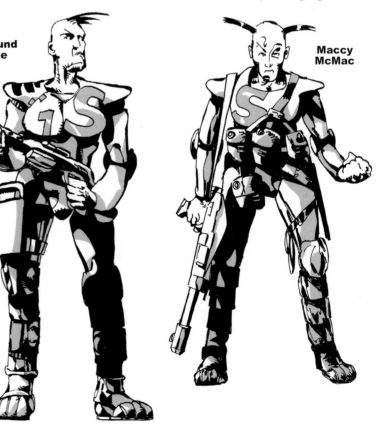

Ozmund Blue

Maccy McMac

neighbouring blocks is just waiting for the Spectres to take a fall so they can pounce on the territory. The citizens of Cher themselves, though suffering constantly from the predations of the gang, have a perverse pride in its existence, for they know full well that no other gang will dare challenge their block while the Spectres are still in control. A Spectre can be identified by the blue sashes they have taken to wearing either on their belts or from a kneepad.

Gang Leader: Ozmund Blue
Lieutenant: Maccy McMac
Base of Operations: Level 12, Cher Sky Rise
Leadership Score: 18
Monthly Income: 95,500 cr.
Gang Members: 120 at 1st level, 14 at 2nd level, 6 at 3rd level, 4 at 4th level, 2 at 5th level, 2 at 6th level

Ozmund Blue

It is probable that the Spectres are now being held together by nothing more than their leader's charismatic personality, for he has few other qualities of leadership. Ozmund Blue (just 'Oz' to his gang members) was nothing more than a cheap punk who managed to rise up the ranks to become a lieutenant in the Spectres through his general brutality and gift for getting juves and other punks to do exactly what he wished. When the last leader of the gang, one Max Sapphire, was arrested for his part in a rumble in the Tweenblock Plaza, Oz slid inexorably into the top slot of the Spectres. In truth, Oz is still a cheap punk and while his followers are fanatically loyal to the gang (it is said no one will dare harm a member) they are only too glad to run rings around their leader if there are a few credits in it for them. For his own part, Oz cares little for such distinctions – he can still rally the entire gang when a rumble or block war is called for and he receives a generous portion of the gang's income, which is pretty much all he desires in life.

Block Champion 4/Citizen 8 (punk); HD 4d8+8d6+27 (76); Init +2 (+2 Dex); Spd 30 ft.; DV 16 (+6 Reflex); Attack +12/+7/+2 las-saw (1d8+2/10), or +12/+7/+2 heavy spit gun (3d6/8); Fort +10, Ref +6, Will +4; Str 15, Dex 12, Con 14, Int 10, Wis 12, Cha 15.
Skills and feats: Appraise +1, Bluff +10, Climb +10, Computer Use +2, Concentration +10, Craze (scrawling) +13, Drive +4, Escape Artist +5, Hide +4, Intimidate +17, Jump +8, Listen +5, Move Silently +9, Sense Motive +8, Streetwise +16, Spot +10, Technical +6; Advanced Leadership, Great Fortitude, Leadership, Lightning Reflexes, Toughness, Weapon Focus (heavy spit gun),

Weapon Proficiency (heavy weapons).
Possessions: Heavy spit gun, las-saw, sports armour (DR 5).

Maccy McMac

Mac acts as both Oz's bodyguard and lieutenant in the Spectres, and the two have remained firm friends over the years. When Oz took leadership of the gang, he made sure his old friend rose with him. Mac is held in little regard by the other members of the gang, for he has an attention to detail that Oz lacks and is a terror for making sure that credits the gang earns stay within the gang rather than the pockets of the punks and juves. The other citizens of the Cher Sky Rise have a much different view of Mac, however, and are keen to support him whenever he takes a more visible role in the Spectre's activities, such as another Tweenblock fight with the Ciccones. There is some pressure from outside of the Spectres for Mac to claim overall leadership, as it is felt that crime against the other citizens in Cher will drop with him in charge and other gangs believe he will be a far easier man to deal with than Oz. While Oz is still alive though, this is unlikely.

Block Champion 2/Bodyguard 5/Citizen 4 (goon)/ Demolitionist 1; HD 5d8+7d6+15 (65); Init +7 (+3 Dex, +4 Improved Initiative); Spd 30 ft.; DV 20 (+10 Reflex); Attack +11/+6/+1 las-knife (1d6+1/10), or +14/+9/+4 sonic blaster (1d10/-); Fort +8, Ref +10, Will +3; Str 13, Dex 16, Con 12, Int 11, Wis 12, Cha 12.
Skills and feats: Climb +5, Computer Use +4, Concentration +9, Hide +5, Intimidate +13, Listen +5, Medical +3, Profession (demolitionist) +13, Sense Motive +16, Streetwise +16, Spot +16, Technical +16; Alertness, Great Fortitude, Improved Initiative, Point Blank Shot, Skill Focus (technical), Toughness, Weapon Focus (sonic blaster).
Possessions: 5 Hi-ex packs, las-knife, sonic blaster, sports armour (DR 5).

The XY Girls

Though tiny in comparison to the Spectres, the XY Girls have gained an enviable amount of notoriety in the area surrounding the Cher Sky Rise, no doubt due to every member being female. An encounter with the XY Girls, however, will be enough to convince even the toughest street punk that these girls are no less formidable than any other gang. The gang's leader, Cleo Patty, jealously coverts every female member of rival gangs and openly makes calls for them to join her, which has led to some friction in the past – especially as the XY Girls are known to despise female punks and juves who serve under a male leadership more than the actual males themselves. This aside, the XY Girls have little contact with other gangs, unless their 'business' interests coincide. They concentrate heavily on burglary, petty thievery and shop-lifting with the single aim of trying to amass as many credits as they possibly can. This money is typically used to fund weaponry for the small gang but also serves to keep every member in the very latest of fashions. The XY Girl's main targets are the citizens and shopping mall of Madonna Ciccone but they will sometimes try their luck against other gangs, if they believe they can get away with it. This has brought them into direct confrontation with the Ciccones, but the XY Girls know that a few feminine wiles can go a long way, and many of their members have been able to walk straight out of Madonna Ciccone, even when caught red-handed by the security guards.

Cleo Patty

Beula Rockintyre

Gang Leader: Cleo Patty
Lieutenant: Beula Rockintyre
Base of Operations: Level 163, Cher Sky Rise
Leadership Score: 11
Monthly Income: 16,500 cr.
Gang Members: 15 at 1st level, 2 at 2nd level

Cleo Patty

As leader of the XY Girls, Cleo has demonstrated an unusual degree of competence and discipline as the head of a street gang. She takes pains never to provoke a gang larger then hers and steers well clear of any conflict with the Justice Department. All her girls are well paid for their activities and so few ever leave the gang. Leaving any heavy or combat-orientated work to her lieutenant, Beula, Cleo concentrates on a variety of credit-making enterprises, revolving around petty theft and shoplifting. Keen to avoid the aggressive attentions of some of the Spectre gang members, she concentrates the XY Girls' activities on Madonna Ciccone block and, given there are only eighteen members in her gang, manages to provide a healthy income for all. Cleo encourages all her girls to use their 'attributes and talent' to escape prosecution

when caught thieving or shoplifting but she is clever enough to never try this on a judge.

Bat Burglar 4/Citizen 3 (dunk); HD 7d6 (27); Init +2 (+2 Dex); Spd 30 ft.; DV 20 (+10 Reflex); Attack +4 knife (1d6-1/2), or +7/+2 laser pistol (4d6/14); Fort +2, Ref +10, Will +3; Str 9, Dex 15, Con 10, Int 14, Wis 13, Cha 17.
Skills and feats: Appraise +6, Bluff +13, Climb +7, Computer Use +7, Concentration +2, Craze (batgliding) +12, Hide +8, Intimidate +11, Jump +5, Listen +7, Medical +3, Move Silently +8, Pick Pocket +14, Search +7, Sense Motive +7, Streetwise +9, Spot +5, Technical +6; Dodge, Leadership, Lightning Reflexes, Skill Focus (pick pocket).
Possessions: Bat-glider, knife, laser pistol, pad armour (DR 4).

Beula Rockintyre

Her nickname, 'a ton of bad news', is perhaps a little unfair as she is no fattie, but Beula's reputation as the heavyweight of the XY Girls is well-founded among the other gangs in the area. The brains of the XY Girls firmly resides with their leader, who relies on Beula to resolve any problem that calls for brawn instead. In this, Beula is most competent. With a physique that puts most toughened male punks to shame, there are few who willing cross Beula unless they outnumber her by at least ten to one. It is an oft-quoted rumour that Beula seeks to challenge Cleo for leadership of the XY Girls, a match that, if it came to physical blows, might be all too one-sided. The gang members, however, do extremely well under Cleo's leadership and it must be clear, even to the meanest brain, that they will be unlikely to follow anyone else.

Citizen 7 (punk); HD 7d6+21 (56); Init +1 (+1 Dex); Spd 30 ft.; DV 13 (+3 Reflex); Attack +9/+4 las-burner (2d12+4/15), or +6/+1 lazooka (5d10/20); Fort +7, Ref +3, Will +1; Str 19, Dex 13, Con 17, Int 7, Wis 9, Cha 13. *Skills and feats:* Bluff +5, Climb +10, Concentration +6, Drive +9, Intimidate +11, Jump +10, Listen +7, Sense Motive +7, Streetwise +5, Spot +6, Technical +2; Endurance, Great Fortitude, Toughness, Weapon Proficiency (heavy weapons). *Possessions:* 4 Hand bombs, las-burner, lazooka, shell jacket (DR 8).

The Wraiths of Wrath

The Wraiths are a relatively new gang in the Cher Sky Rise and have benefited in the past from disaffected Spectre members joining their ranks, especially when Oz took control of the larger gang. The members of the Wraiths fully believe it is their right and destiny to grow larger than the Spectres, challenge them and gain full control of the sky rise. To those outside, this is a ludicrous dream, for while the Wraith's leader, Dreemo Knight, has done well to climb above all the other gangs, there is simply too much distance between his men and the Spectres – if the Spectres are to fall, it will likely come about because of their own bad decisions and luck, rather than being forced out by another gang. Many skirmishes have taken place between the two gangs throughout

the past few months and the Wraiths have managed to interfere enough with some of the Spectres' operations that even Ozmund Blue is beginning to take an interest in forcing them out of Cher Sky Rise for good. The other citizens of the block know a big confrontation is coming soon – it is just a question of who will move first.

Gang Leader: Dreemo Knight
Lieutenant: Lance Devero
Base of Operations: Level 49, Cher Sky Rise
Leadership Score: 12
Monthly Income: 23,500 cr.
Gang Members: 20 at 1st level, 2 at 2nd level, 1 at 3rd level

Dreemo Knight

Dreemo is a perfect example of a man who wants everything yesterday and it is all too apparent that his gang suffers because of his demands. Having once set himself up as a self-styled, not to say unsuccessful,

Dreemo Knight

Lance Devero

assassin, he quickly found that it was far easier to let others do the work and take the risks, while he could simply sit back and 'supervise' them. He pulled the Wraiths together after seeing how effective the Spectres were at controlling their territory. Though he knows the Spectres still far outweigh his gang in terms of both manpower and resources Dreemo believes, perhaps foolishly, that the day of the Wraiths is coming and that he will soon occupy the top slot at Cher Sky Rise.

Assassin 1/Citizen 8 (juve); HD 6d6+9 (32); Init +0; Spd 30 ft.; DV 14 (+4 Reflex); Attack +8/+3 knife (1d6+1/2), or +8/+3 high velocity rifle (3d6/14); Fort +3, Ref +4, Will +1; Str 13, Dex 11, Con 12, Int 9, Wis 8, Cha 12.
Skills and feats: Bluff +7, Climb +5, Computer Use +8, Concentration +7, Craze (boinging) +4, Drive +11, Hide +8, Intimidate +6, Jump +5, Medical +4, Move Silently +8, Pilot +6, Sense Motive +3, Streetwise +5, Technical +3; Far Shot, Leadership, Point Blank Shot, Skill Focus (streetwise), Weapon Focus (high velocity rifle).
Possessions: High velocity rifle, knife, pad armour (DR 4).

Lance Devero

To all intents and purposes, Lance is a gifted lieutenant to his leader Dreemo Knight and has been rewarded well for his efforts in securing a foothold for the Wraiths in Cher Sky Rise. Lance, however, is all too aware of the course of destruction that his leader has set for the gang, and is actively plotting against Dreemo with Maccy McMac. Planning to betray Dreemo to the Spectres and take his place as leader of the Wraiths, Lance firmly believes the future for 'his' gang involves working with, not against, the Spectres. He is confident that no-one else yet suspects what he is up to and has begun to co-ordinate his own criminal operations, thus getting the other gang members used to taking orders directly from him, rather than always listening to Dreemo. He has also recently been recruited by Judge Sparque to act as her nark, something Lance foolishly believes will benefit him even further – after all, with the Justice Department on his side, how can he possibly fail to gain leadership of his gang?

Citizen 7 (jugger driver)/Nark 1; HD 8d6+8 (38); Init +0; Spd 30 ft.; DV 12 (+2 Reflex); Attack +6 knife (1d6/2), or +5 spit pistol (2d6/6); Fort +3, Ref +2, Will +3; Str 13, Dex 10, Con 13, Int 9, Wis 8, Cha 11.
Skills and feats: Bluff +10, Computer Use +9, Drive +13, Hide +4, Intimidate +5, Jump +3, Knowledge (sector 190) +9, Listen +3, Medical +2, Sense Motive +5, Streetwise +11, Spot +3, Technical +8; Luck of Grud, Point Blank Shot, Run, Skill Focus (drive), Skill Focus (streetwise).
Possessions: Knife, pad armour (DR 4), spit pistol.

The Spug-Offs

A juve gang based in Cher Sky Rise, the Spug-Offs are more a nuisance to the other gangs than anything else and are typically treated with extreme condescension. Not that this bothers the juves – as far as they are concerned, the whole city is against them and they have everything to prove, both to themselves and the other citizens of the sky rise. With regular run-ins with the patrol judges of the area, the Spug-Offs spend most of their time hanging around the Tweenblock Plaza and the shopping malls of both Cher and Madonna Ciccone, generally making a lot of noise and intimidating citizens passing by. They have little in the way of serious criminal interests, content to simply take what they want, when they want it. Most of the stolen ground cars that go missing from the vehicle parks of both blocks can generally be attributed to the Spug-Offs but so far most members have been lucky enough to avoid any serious time in the juve-cubes.

Gang Leader: Marvin Thorpe
Lieutenant: Rahji Nath
Base of Operations: Tweenblock Plaza, Cher Sky Rise and Madonna Ciccone
Leadership Score: 7
Monthly Income: 4,500 cr.
Gang Members: 5 at 1st level

Marvin Thorpe

Though several years before his time, Marvin idolises Chopper as living proof of just what a juve in the Big Meg can achieve when his mind is set to the task. Unfortunately, Marvin has little natural talent in skysurfing, or any other sport for that matter, and so gathered a number of juves of Cher Sky Rise that have not already fallen under the leadership of the larger gangs. Marvin's leadership qualities are enough to stop the other juves straying, but he provides little real direction other than coming up with more pranks and egging his members on to steal this ground car or that jewelled kneepad. The closest thing to a friend that he has is his lieutenant, Rahji Nath, but even Marvin can feel a little queasy if he spends too much time in the company of the immigrant. Marvin's notoriety within his own gang crept up a few notches when he managed to steal a zip gun from a Spectre gang member, the only real weapon the Spug-Offs possess.

Marvin Thorpe

Rahji Nath

Citizen 6 (juve); HD 6d6 (23); Init +2 (+2 Dex); Spd 30 ft.; DV 14 (+4 Reflex); Attack +4 club (1d8/10), or +6/+1 zip gun (2d8/4); Fort +2, Ref +4, Will +2; Str 11, Dex 14, Con 10, Int 11, Wis 10, Cha 13.
Skills and feats: Computer Use +2, Craze (boinging) +9, Craze (jetpacking) +8, Craze (jet sticking) +6, Craze (scrawling) +11, Drive +10, Hide +10, Intimidate +7, Jump +7, Listen +7, Streetwise +11, Spot +6, Technical +2; Improved Resist Arrest, Leadership, Luck of Grud, Resist Arrest, Skill Focus (streetwise).
Possessions: Club, pad armour (DR 4), zip gun.

Rahji Nath

An immigrant from Indo-Cit, Rahji has always been treated as an outsider since his arrival in Mega-City One and has grown used to solitude. He appreciates Marvin's attempts to bring him into the Spug-Offs but forever fears discovery of his greatest secret – Rahji is a rogue psyker, having slipped through the standard immigration checks as he entered the city. He uses his supernatural powers only when absolutely necessary but has not been able to escape the stigma of citizens just sensing something is 'wrong' with him. In a way, he is lucky to be an immigrant, for most simply put down their discomfort in his presence to him being a foreigner, but some of the other juves in the Spug-Offs have begun to notice that

Rahji always does his best to leave the area whenever a judge is close by.

Citizen 6 (rogue psyker); HD 6d6 (22); Init +1 (+1 Dex); Spd 30 ft.; DV 13 (+3 Reflex); Attack +3 knife (1d6-1/2), or +5 knife (1d6-1/2); Fort +2, Ref +3, Will +6; Str 8, Dex 12, Con 10, Int 10, Wis 14, Cha 13.
Skills and feats: Bluff +3, Climb +3, Computer Use +4, Concentration +9, Craze (scrawling) +8, Drive +3, Hide +8, Intimidate +3, Jump +3, Knowledge (psi-talent) +9, Listen +11, Medical +5, Sense Motive +11, Streetwise +8, Spot +8, Technical +2; Alertness, Inner Strength, Iron Will, Talented.
Power Points: 20.
Psi-Powers: 0-level: *detect psi-talent, inkling, mind shield;* 1st level: *psychometry, telempathic projection;* 2nd level: *detect thoughts.*
Possessions: Knife, 2 smoke bombs.

Old Age Citizens Protection League

Life can be extremely tough for a centenarian in Mega-City One, particularly if they live in a place like Cher Sky Rise. A small number of eldsters have banded together for mutual protection and have proved extremely successful – muggings on older citizens have dropped in the sky rise and more eldsters are joining the Old Age Citizens Protection League (OACPL). Though the gang started off by simply arranging common times to be in the hallways of Cher Sky Rise, so that none would ever face a group of juves alone, the OACPL has since become 'pro-active'. The gang now prowls the hallways of Cher, armed with a rather surprising array of weaponry (their combined savings provide a healthy income for the gang), primarily attacking lone juves, though any thug or goon is a viable target. Several have been arrested and sentenced to the cubes for assault and the eldsters have been creating an incredible amount of friction with the other gangs in the block. Much to the chagrin of the Spectres and Wraiths, however, it seems that no matter how many eldsters they hasten to a 'natural' death, more always seem ready to join the fight. It seems the more eldsters feel oppressed by another one of their number being attacked by a perp (no matter who started the fight), the more they are ready to sign up to the OACPL.

Gang Leader: Arthur Lomez
Lieutenant: Buster Rodgers

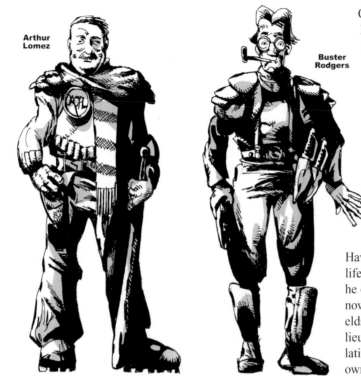

Arthur Lomez

Buster Rodgers

Citizen 9 (med-tech); HD 9d6-18 (23); Init -1 (-1 Dex); Spd 30 ft.; DV 14 (+4 Reflex); Attack +4 club (1d8-2/0), or +5 hand gun (3d6/4); Fort +1, Ref +4, Will +8; Str 6, Dex 9, Con 7, Int 14, Wis 16, Cha 17. *Skills and feats:* Appraise +9, Bluff +10, Climb +2, Computer Use +14, Concentration +4, Craze (sex) +7, Drive +5, Hide +6, Intimidate +15, Jump +2, Listen +12, Medical +17, Pilot +2, Sense Motive +13, Streetwise +15, Spot +7, Technical +10; Blind-Fight, Iron Will, Leadership, Lightning Reflexes, Skill Focus (medical). *Possessions:* Club, hand gun, silencer, shell jacket (DR 8).

Buster Rodgers

Having been in trouble with the Law for most of his adult life, Buster was a natural recruit to the OACPL. Whereas he once cursed his growing frailty and old age, he has now received a new lease of life by protecting the other eldsters of his home block. Though technically the lieutenant of the OACPL, Buster enjoys a great deal of latitude from Art and plans many 'juve-sweeps' on his own and, in turn, is always keen to listen to ideas other eldsters of the gang may come up with to make their block a safer place for the elderly. Most members see Buster as the natural choice to take over the leadership of the OACPL when Art is finally arrested once more though it is all too likely that Buster's own violent actions in the hallways of the block will land him in the cubes before his leader.

Citizen 10 (agitator); HD 10d6+3 (41); Init +1 (+1 Dex); Spd 30 ft.; DV 11 (+1 Reflex); Attack +8/+3 las-knife (1d6+1/10), or +5 zip gun (2d8/4); Fort +5, Ref +1, Will +5; Str 12, Dex 6, Con 10, Int 12, Wis 15, Cha 13. *Skills and feats:* Appraise +3, Bluff +8, Climb +5, Computer Use +6, Concentration +6, Craze (batgliding) +10, Drive +7, Hide +3, Intimidate +14, Jump +5, Listen +12, Medical +6, Pilot +7, Sense Motive +9, Streetwise +15, Spot +14, Technical +9; Endurance, Great Fortitude, Resist Arrest, Toughness, Two Weapon Fighting. *Possessions:* 2 Las-knives, pad armour (DR 4), zip gun.

The Ciccones

Though few citizens have lived in the Madonna Ciccone cityblock long enough to form any real ties with either the block itself or any gangs, there is a growing recognition that they have moved into 'hostile' territory. The citizens of several neighbouring blocks are growing

Base of Operations: Level 99, Cher Sky Rise
Leadership Score: 15
Monthly Income: 26,000 cr.
Gang Members: 35 at 1st level, 4 at 2nd level, 1 at 3rd level, 1 at 4th level

Arthur Lomez

Art to his comrades in arms, Lomez was the original founder of the OACPL and, despite several attempts on his life, has displayed an incredible degree of luck and resilience to have survived this long. A life-long pacifist, Art has become the most militant of eldsters in the Cher Sky Rise after having lost his wife to a vicious mugging – the judges were never able to discover who the perps were. Taking the Law into his own hands, Art gathered his closest friends and pounced on the first group of juves they came across. Their heroic actions left seven juves in need of medical care and captured the imagination of many eldsters who had previously resigned themselves to live out their dwindling lives in fear. Though many of the local patrol judges are sympathetic to his cause, they are required to come down heavily on any vigilante group – Art has done his share of time in the cubes and is looking at an additional repeat offence charge should he ever be arrested again. He remains stubbornly defiant, however, and is sure that even if he falls, others will pick up the leadership of the OACPL and carry on the good work.

increasingly jealous of Ciccone's relatively luxurious living space but none so much as the residents of Cher Sky Rise. Some of the victims of crime within Madonna Ciccone have since banded together in order to stake their own claim in the area though it is all too apparent that the noble aspirations of the leader, Lexx Looker, are being quickly eroded by those who see Madonna Ciccone as 'virgin territory', ripe for exploitation through protection rackets, slabwalkers and other illegal interests.

Gang Leader: Lexx Looker
Lieutenant: Brass Gixgy
Base of Operations: Level 202, Madonna Ciccone
Leadership Score: 10
Monthly Income: 10,500 cr.
Gang Members: 10 at 1st level, 1 at 2nd level

Lexx Looker

When he first started recruiting for his gang, Lexx was determined that the Ciccones would be every bit as large and powerful as the Spectres of Cher Sky Rise. Fate and a fractious group have both conspired to all but destroy his dreams and now Lexx is barely capable of stopping his people from preying on the other residents of Madonna Ciccone, rather than concentrate on the 'enemy' in Cher Sky Rise. In particular, he has had trouble with his lieutenant, Brass Gixgy, who has all but openly challenged his leadership and is at the head of the Ciccone's most profitable (and most illegal) operations. Lexx is struggling to retain control of his dream, but it is steadily being taken away from him.

Citizen 7 (vigilante); HD 7d6 (27); Init +1 (+1 Dex); Spd 30 ft.; DV 13 (+3 Reflex); Attack +5 las-knife (1d6-1/10), or +7/+2 laser pistol (4d6/14); Fort +2, Ref +3, Will +2; Str 9, Dex 12, Con 11, Int 10, Wis 11, Cha 12.
Skills and feats: Appraise +8, Bluff +8, Climb +5, Computer Use +10, Concentration +6, Drive +5, Hide +5, Intimidate +7, Jump +4, Listen +8, Medical +8, Pilot +3, Sense Motive +4, Streetwise +4, Spot +9, Technical +5; Alertness, Control Crash, Leadership, Skill Focus (intimidate), Track.
Possessions: Las-knife, laser pistol, pad armour (DR 4).

Brass Gixgy

Through his connections with the Madonna Ciccone Citi-Def unit, Gixgy has shot up in the ranks of the Ciccones. Once valued by Lexx as a man who could potentially bring the respectable firepower of the Citi-Def into any confrontation with rival gangs, he is now treated with extreme suspicion as Gixgy has only used his influence to solidify his own position. Now running more illegal rackets than Lexx can ever guess at, it is Gixgy who holds the purse strings to all the credits the Ciccones bring in and it can now only be a matter of time before Lexx is disposed of and Gixgy takes the lead in a brand new criminal organisation.

Citizen 7 (Citi-Def soldier); HD 7d6+14 (41); Init +2 (+2 Dex); Spd 30 ft.; DV 14 (+4 Reflex); Attack +7/+2 las-saw (1d8+1/10), or +8/+3 laser rifle (4d8/14); Fort +4, Ref +4, Will +1; Str 12, Dex 14, Con 14, Int 12, Wis 9, Cha 14.
Skills and feats: Bluff +12, Climb +7, Computer Use +8, Concentration +9, Drive +6, Hide +6, Intimidate +12, Jump +7, Knowledge (military) +7, Listen +3, Medical +1, Pilot +6, Sense Motive +7, Streetwise +9, Spot +3, Technical +9; Leadership, Resist Arrest, Weapon Focus (las-saw), Weapon Focus (laser rifle).
Possessions: Las-saw, laser rifle, shell jacket (DR 8).

Lex Looker

Brass Gixgy

Rules Summary

Unit Hit Points

Majority of unit has Toughness feat	+10%
Unit has Constitution ability score modifier	+/-10% per Con modifier
Majority of unit are judges	+25%

Ranged Attacks Against Units

Unit Size	Attack Roll Modifier
6-10	+1
11-20	+2
21-50	+5
51-100	+7
101-200	+9
201or more	Automatic Hit

Outmatching

Unit Size is. . .	Attack Roll Modifier	Damage Roll Modifier	Morale Modifier
Ten times or more then enemy's	+5	X 10	+5
Five times enemy's	+3	X 5	+3
Three times enemy's	+2	X 3	+2
Twice enemy's	+1	X 2	+1
Less than twice but more than 50% of enemy's	+0	-	+0
50% of enemy's	-1	X 1	-1
33% of enemy's	-2	X 1	-2
20% of enemy's	-3	X 1	-3
10% or less of enemy's	-5	X ½	-5

Ranged Damage Modifiers

Unit Size of Attacker	Damage Modifier
6-10	-
11-20	-
21-50	-
51-100	X 2
101-200	X 3
201-500	X 4
501-1,000	X 5
1,001-2,500	X 8
2,501-5,000	X 12
5,001-10,000	X 15
10,001 or more	X 20

Area Effect Damage Modifiers

Area Effect	Damage Modifier
5 ft.	X 1½
10 ft.	X 4
15 ft.	X 8
20 ft.	X 10
30 ft.	X 15
60 ft.	X 20
100 ft.	X 40
Cone	Additional x2

Morale Checks

Morale Circumstance	Morale check DC
Unit Hit Points reduced to half of original score	15
Unit Hit Points reduced to one quarter of original score	10
Unit in melee combat suffers more damage in a round than enemy	15
Unit suffers a hit from an enemy of three times or greater Unit Hit Points	15
Unit withdraws from combat	20

Morale Modifiers

Morale	Modifier
Unit has no leader	-4
Unit Leader	+ Leader's Charisma modifier
Morale modifier*	+/- Morale modifier
Unit Leader has Leadership feat	+ Leader's Character Level
Player actions	See p25

Mass Arrests

Circumstance	Mass Arrest check Modifier
Every Pat-Wagon or H-Wagon in sight of unit	+2
Every Manta Prowl Tank in sight of unit	+3
Unit in cover	-5
Unit involved in combat	-2
Unit already faced Mass Arrest check	-5
Judge has 10 or more ranks in Intimidate	+2
Unit reduced to half original unit hit points or less	+2

Player Actions

Player Action	Morale Bonus to Unit
Slaying enemy unit leader	+2
Destroying enemy vehicle	+3
Fleeing battle	-4
Slaying 10% or more of enemy unit in one attack	+1

Recovering Casualties

Character with at least 4 ranks in Medical skill present	+1% per character (max. +20%)
Unit withdrew from melee combat	-20%
Unit possess the Improved Recover feat	+10%

Unit and Vehicle Roster Sheets

Unit Name:

Class: **Level:**   **Unit Size:**

Unit Hit Points:

Unit Leader:

Initiative: **Attacks:**   **Damage:**

DV:

Damage Reduction:

Special Abilities:

Ability Scores: Str   Dex   Con   Int   Wis   Cha

Saves: Fort   Ref   Will

Feats:

Vehicle Name:

Vehicle:

Hit Points:

Attacks:

Damage:

DV:

Damage Reduction: